THE
MARRIAGE-GO-ROUND

An Exploratory Study of Multiple Marriage

Elaine Fox

WITHDRAWN

UNIVERSITY
PRESS OF
AMERICA

LANHAM • NEW YORK • LONDON

Copyright © 1983 by

University Press of America,™ Inc.

4720 Boston Way
Lanham, MD 20706

3 Henrietta Street
London WC2E 8LU England

Library of Congress Cataloging in Publication Data

Fox, Elaine, 1947–
  The marriage–go–round.

  Bibliography: p.
  1. Divorce–United States. 2. Remarriage–United
States. I. Title.
HQ834.F69   1983   306.8'4   83–12405
ISBN 0–8191–3376–0
ISBN 0–8191–3377–9 (pbk. : alk. paper)

For

Ken Kiser,

advisor, mentor and friend.

CONTENTS

LIST OF TABLES

CHAPTER I

THE STUDY OF DIVORCE

Introduction

In the past few decades we have seen the United States experiment in many alternative family forms. There has been an increase in cohabitation, communal formation, limitation of family size, dual career marriage, heightened stress on sexuality, and rapidly rising divorce rates to name but a few of the major changes. Each increase in the incidence of these categories has seen a polarization of response. The "me first" generation usually greets each rise with glee and proclaims that individuality is finally flourishing. The opposing camp sadly shakes its head and mutters phrases about the death of the American family.

It is moot to argue whether these changes are good or bad, for the essential fact is they do exist and the best we can do is gain an understanding of each phenomenon by intensive research. This has been the primary response of social scientists with one exception. Little substantive research has been undertaken in the field of remarriage and divorce. The classics in the area (Goode, 1956; Bernard, 1956; Westoff, 1975; Hunt and Hunt, 1966, 1974) stand alone as exemplary examples of in-depth studies of a rising phenomenon with few other researchers producing work in the area. Investigation into the area of remarriage and divorce must be pieced together from journal articles published in a wide array of professional interests from anthropology to social work.

Research into the area of remarriage and divorce has primarily concentrated on the period of adjustment from termination of the first marriage until entrance into the second or in comparisons between first and second marriages with regard to homogamous variables, interaction patterns and inherent problems. Almost no research has been done specifically in the area of sequential marriage, often referred to as serial monogamy.

Remarriage after divorce is an emerging phenomenon. Price and Balswick (1980) suggest that remarriages represent 32% of all marriages in the United States with Glick and Norton (1976) estimating that eventually

1

80% of all individuals currently divorcing will remarry. Hidden within the demographic findings describing the incidence of remarriage after divorce are the
small, but growing, number of individuals engaging in
multiple divorce and remarriage. According to Westoff
(1975) almost six per cent of all marriages are composed of those persons who are presently engaged in
at least a third marriage. Glick and Norton (1977)
suggest that serial marriage is less prevalent. They
indicate that for each "100 first marriages, 38 will
end in divorce. Of the 38 divorces, three-fourths
(29) will remarry. Of the 29 who remarry, 44 per cent,
or 13, will become redivorced" (p. 26). Estimates of
serial monogamy generally set the incidence at around
two to three percent of all marriages.

The initial response of the public to questions
of multiple marriage is one of denial or astonishment.
"I don't know anyone like that" or "Why in heaven
would anyone get married that many times?" are the
typical reactions. To the first response I would
simply ask for reflective thought. There is a more
than good chance that everyone does know of someone
who is divorced from a second marriage or is engaged
in a third. Multiple marriers do exist.

The question as to why someone would want to
remarry numerous times is more difficult to answer.
It involves a response which must take into account
many factors and varying perspectives. All too often
additional questions rather than resolutions are
generated by the inquiry into serial marriage. A
brief review of these various factors and perspectives
will be undertaken shortly. Prior to exploring the
process of multiple marriage, however, it is first
necessary to have a basic understanding of the contributing elements involved in divorce in general, for
most certainly one time divorce and multiple divorce
share commonalities.

Divorce as a Cultural Experience

Goode (1962), in a cross-cultural analysis of
divorce rates, suggests that divorce may be theoretically conceptualized as a failure of boundary-
maintaining forces. He points out several institutional patterns societies may utilize as a mechanism
for coping with potential or real marital strain in

order to prevent a high divorce rate. The first of
these patterns involves the lowering of societal
expectations for the emotional rewards of the marriage
relationship. In other words, persons are socialized
into not expecting a high degree of emotional bonding
between spouses, thus insuring that termination of
the marriage will not occur as a result of alienation
between the dyad stemming from inadequate emotional
need fulfillment. This technique of social control
of marital conflict is practiced and found to be
highly effective in other cultures but is not so in
ours.

According to Parsons (1955), the specialized
function of the American family has focused on emotional fulfillment and we tend to teach our children to
expect the marital relationship to be the one viable
institution where need fulfillment can be obtained.
As Bernard (1956) explains, we are so socialized into
accepting marriage as the primary form of emotional
attachment to someone that only those individuals not
fully qualified for marriage (i.e., the chronically
ill, the disfigured, etc.) primarily account for the
small numbers of Americans who don't marry. Although
this is a changing phenomenon due to liberalization of
the female role in society, it is still overwhelmingly
true for the large majority of Americans.

Most Americans marry at some time during their
lives. Ninety-four percent of all men and 96 percent
of all women marry by the time they have reached
their early fifties (Glick, 1978). We enter our first
marriage with high expectations for marital bliss and
when that marriage fails, we seek out another. Most
divorced persons remarry within a three year time span
from time of divorce and those individuals who do not
remarry are generally female and remain single not
from choice but from a vastly reduced pool of eligibles
(Spanier and Glick, 1980). Thus while people may
object to one particular marriage, the argument is not
with marriage as an institution. As Jones (1978)
points out, the very high remarriage rate of the
divorced suggests that divorce implies disillusionment
with a specific marriage, but not marriage per se. We
enter our second marriages with perhaps only slightly
tarnished expectations. A conclusion which may be
drawn from the rapid rate with which we remarry is
that marital disharmony is not controlled at a societal
level by a reduction in marital expectations.

Goode (1962), in his analysis of divorce, goes on to state that marital instability can be controlled by placing the greatest social values on the kinship network thus reducing the importance of the husband-wife relationship. While this procedure may again be effective in other cultures it fails dramatically in ours. We highly value the integrity of the dyad, often to the exclusion of other kinship ties. This factor manifests itself in several ways. The newly married couple is expected to stand on their own and even if financial aid is received from the parents, an economic investment in the newly formed dyad does not buy parents a right to participate in decision making for the children. Any well-intentioned advice is often seen as an invasion of privacy by the young married couple.

Further evidence of the importance of the husband-wife relationship can be seen in the manner in which we achieve social standing on the part of the female. A female's social standing, regardless of her family background, is still obtained by and assumed determined by her husband's position in the social strata (Nilson, 1976) despite the fact that she may be engaging in a career of her own.

Emphasis on the importance of the husband-wife relationship is also seen in other aspects of American society. While prejudice for the divorced and single female head of household has shown signs of decreasing in the past decade as evidenced by movements toward equalization of credit and job opportunities, such terms as "fatherless children" and "broken home" designate the degree of stigmatization still present. Stigma is ascribed to divorced and separated women for their presumed inability to keep their men (Brandwein, 1974). Again, the importance of the husband-wife relationship is reinforced.

Furthermore, females who divorce seldom return home to the household of their parents and while occasional financial aid is extended, most females are expected to make it on their own. There is no reopening of the parental nest for immediate incorporation of the divorced daughter and her children. The American family in today's society is nuclear (Current Pop. Reports #297, 1976).

American society is organized to stress the importance of the husband-wife relationship and to allow for a loosening of ties with kin network, whether it be parents or siblings. We don't control marital instability in this society by emphasis on kinship.

A third element utilized by Goode (1962) in his analysis of the curtailment of marital instability is the implementation of homogamy as a prerequisite for marriage. Most societies reduce potential stress by insuring that the husband-wife dyad have similar backgrounds. While a process of mate selection based on complementary needs may be effective to a large extent, it is not a pervasive phenomenon and cannot be considered a totally effective means of social control in mate selection (Winch, 1971). In a society which values upward mobility it is often necessary for the young to leave their home of origin in order to seek advancement in other geographical areas. This separation from the parental home negates mate selection as a function of kinship guidance and thus reduces the influence of homogamy which would be emphasized by the parents. In this society we stress love as the basis for marriage and although we generally agree that married spouses should be closely aligned in terms of interests and social backgrounds we still consider romantic the stories of the princess and the plumber.

By this brief summary of Goode's (1962) analysis of cultural mechanisms for controlling marital instability we can understand that the United States does not practice strict control measures which might insure a low rate of marital dissolution while at the same time neither do we institutionalize practices which encourage marital dissolution.

> Divorce is one of the major solutions for an
> intense degree of marital disharmony and is to
> be found in most societies and nations. Yet
> I know of no contemporary society, primitive
> or industrialized, in which divorce is actually
> valued. Divorce has its consequences for the
> society, the kin networks, and the individual;
> and these are tedious when not awkward, and
> burdensome when not destructive (p. 513)

While we may not necessarily value divorce as an entity, we do accept its existence as a necessary evil and cure-all for problems between two individuals in a particular marriage. One's own divorce and per-

5

haps one's sister's divorce can often be successfully rationalized as the only possible answer to a high level of marital unhappiness without undue concern, but when we begin to examine national statistics on divorce as a whole we begin to understand the overwhelming impact of "everyone's" divorce.

The past two decades have seen an increase in the rate of divorce. In 1976 there were 90 divorced persons per 1000 population (Figure 1). This shows an increase of 90% from the 1970 ratio when divorced persons accounted for 47 persons per thousand. This figure represents an increase of 157% from 1960 to the present (Glick and Norton, 1976). Stated in other terms, it is estimated that one-third of all marriages will end in divorce and four-fifths of these divorced persons will remarry. Even higher rates of divorce are predicted for those in the cohort age group of twenty to thirty. "As persons now in their twenties and thirties survive past middle age, they will probably display an ever higher level of total remarriage experience than persons now in the older age cohorts" (Spanier and Glick, 1980, p. 283). The implication of such mass divorce can be estimated in financial costs in the millions but the emotional costs in terms of stress due to termination of marriage and disrupted households cannot be estimated.

Increased divorce rates can be predicted from observation of the state of the society. Statistics indicate that the divorce rates tend to decrease during economic recessions and increase sharply during wars, after which there is a return to the level of prewar trend (Schwartz, 1968). Laner (1978), in an intensive study of divorce rates, correlated the tendency to have high rates of divorce with multifaceted societal changes.

High divorce rate societies were found to be characterized by the following cultural changes: a transition from predominantly sacred to predominantly secular values (Kirkpatrick, 1955); a transition from population homogeneity to heterogeneity (Burgess & Locke, 1953); resulting in high rates of intermarriage (Cavan, 1963); a movement toward equalization of access to divorce-granting agencies, with a concomitant ease of obtaining divorce (Goode, 1962, 1964); a transition to the use of predominantly subjective criteria as the basis for mate selection

6

(Sirjamaki, 1960); a rise in the importance of
the emotional relationship between husband and
wife (Dennis, 1962); and a high expectancy of
affective intensity in the husband-wife relationship (Parsons & Fox, 1960). Another change
is the generally more permissive attitude
toward individual behavior (Chester, 1971).
Finally, there has been a trend toward bilateral
descent, neolocal residence, and the 'independent' nuclear family (Johnson, 1971) (p. 213).

All of the above mentioned cultural factors can be
seen as being in direct opposition with Goode's
analysis of factors which tend to stabilize marriages.
Thus from a rather high level of theoretical generali-
zation we can come to understand the phenomenon of
divorce in the United States as it is influenced by
cultural contributions. In short, we have attempted
to set the stage for a discussion of divorce by reflecting on societal factors which help influence
divorce rates while coexisting with societal values
which do not necessarily hold divorce dear.

Divorce and Remarriage from a

Demographic Perspective

In order to come to a better understanding of the
phenomenon of divorce and remarriage we need to
describe demographically those who engage in these
activities. In contrast to popular views that those
individuals engaging in divorce are persons in their
middle years who have grown disenchanted with their
spouse over many years, we find instead a relatively
young cohort actively divorcing and remarrying. A
rise in the divorce rate during the last decade has
occurred among couples of all ages, but by far the
greatest age-specific rate of increase has taken
place among couples in the range of 25 to 39 years of
age, the range within which three-fifths of all
divorces occur (Current Population Reports, #297,
(1976).

The median interval between first marriage and
divorce is around seven years, whereas the model length
of time between marriage and divorce is two to three
years (Spanier and Glick, 1980). Remarriage occurs
at a rapid rate with the median length of time between

7

divorce and remarriage being about three years with
one-third of remarriages occurring within two years
after divorce. There is a direct relationship between
length of marriage and tendency to remarry. The
shorter the length of the first marriage the greater
the likelihood to remarry soon.

This tendency lends itself to interpretation of
the fact that the younger the age at divorce, the
greater the likelihood to remarry at all as is evidenced in the fact that 60% of divorced women were
under 30 at time of the divorce and they were three
times as likely to remarry within five years as women
who were 40 years or over at time of divorce (Glick,
1978). These facts are correlated with the tendency
of males to remarry more rapidly than females. In
other words, men simply do not stay on the market very
long after a divorce and given the double standard of
aging, men have a much wider selection group than
females.

Women who remain in a first marriage for longer
intervals of time are likely to be older and have more
children when initially divorced and these factors
are hindrances on the road to remarriage. Their pool
of eligibles is considerably diminished. Also
associated with lessened likelihood for remarriage is
high levels of education for women and being black.

From the above discussion of demographic data
pertaining to divorce and remarriage, we should be able
to ascertain characteristics of the multi-marriers. It
appears that multi-marriers should show a tendency to
be male, to have engaged in their first marriage at
a very early age, and to have produced few if any
children from the first marriages. Female multi-
marriers also should show a tendency to have first
married at an early age, have few if any children from
the first or second marriage, possess only average
educational backgrounds, be white and still relatively
young at the time of entrance into the third marriage.
Given the reduced pool of male eligibles a purely
intuitive hunch would predict older categories of
female multi-marriers to be especially attractive.

Reasons for Remarriage

Why do people remarry? After undergoing a grueling

8

first experience with marriage, it is interesting to note why people attempt another possible disastrous experience. Smart (1977) suggests that a need for intimacy is of primary motivation for remarriage. Most persons engaged in second marriages cite companionship and sexual access (Westoff, 1975; Hunt and Hunt, 1977) as being particularly influential in the decision to remarry. These could be classified as positive forces which push people into remarriage.

Negative forces also play a role in decisions to remarry and these forces are as fundamental although not as pleasant as desires to seek intimacy. Brandwein (1974) suggests that stigmatization of divorced females create a coercive influence in women's lives.

The societal myth of the gay divorcee out to seduce other women's husbands leads to social ostracism of the divorced woman and her family. There are expectations of neighbors, schools, and courts that children from broken homes will not be properly disciplined, will have sex role confusion, and will be more likely to get into trouble. The mothers themselves may incorporate society's attitudes, feeling insecure and guilt-ridden regarding their childbearing abilities (p. 499).

Bernard (1956), Goode (1956), Bohannon (1970) support the assumption that the divorced mother may experience great amounts of guilt with regard to her children and Glasser and Navarre (1965) hold the perspective that divorced women believe society sees them as abnormal and deviant and they themselves accept the label. Spanier and Casto (1979) in their analysis of separation and divorce show that lack of support from friends or family increases the overall difficulties in adjusting to separation and divorce. This lack of support may push individuals into rapid remarriage. Brandwein (1974) also asserts that there are few social support systems operating in society for the divorced, particularly for the divorced female with children.

While it is true that companionship, intimacy, and sexual accessibility can be found outside the marital relationship, such arrangements, if made public, are often open to criticism (Bernard, 1956) and this public information may certainly lead to further stigmatization of the divorced person. Hunt and Hunt (1977) cite financial security as a possible motivating factor in

9

remarriage and for many females living on minimal income this can be a highly influencial factor. As Brandwein (1974) explains, poverty and divorce are highly related.

What we find, then, are many reasons pushing people into remarriage. Remarriage for some may be considered an escape from societal pressures (Goode, 1956) rather than a carefree journey into matrimonial bliss. Many facets of stigmatization associated with divorce in the past have been lifted in the last decade to a certain extent but coercive pressure is still evidenced. Divorce has not been completely institutionalized in society as yet.

In essence, remarriage may be undertaken for a combination of reasons, with both positive and negative forces operating on the individual simultaneously. In short, remarriage may be seen as an attempt to regain feelings of self-worth (Duberman, 1976), to be readmitted to an accredited social institution (Schlesinger, 1970) as the most viable symbol of commitment in a relationship (Garfield, 1980) as well as a mechanism for escape from a precarious social situation.

Mate Selection and Marriage the Second Time Around

It is a common adage in American society that divorced persons remarry someone exactly like their first mate and that subsequent marriages are repetitions of first marriages (Bitterman, 1968). This suggestion has not necessarily been proven to be true. Peters (1976) in a comparison of mate selection and marriages in a sample of the remarried divorced found that females sought different characteristics in their second husbands and indeed the marriages were rated by the participants as being different. According to this study and others (Albrecht, 1979; Westoff, 1975; Hunt and Hunt, 1977; Schlesinger, 1970) there are perceptible differences between first and second marriages. Freer sexual expression, more open communication, and more depth to companionship are often cited by remarried persons.

Dean and Gurak (1978) suggest there is less homogamy present in second marriages which may simply reflect the marriage market realities of a smaller and more heterogeneous mate pool. Although, as Peters (1976) points out, some doubt at marriage is inevitable due to the very nature of the risk and unpredictability of marriage, most couples rate the first year of remarriage as happier than the first year of the initial marriage.

Remarriages have a higher divorce rate than first marriages and this statistic has often been interpreted as being indicative of instability in remarriage. Implied in this assumption is that second marriages are also unhappier. Glenn (1977) prefers to interpret this statistic differently. From his perspective, rates of marriage instability cannot be equated with rates of happiness of those marriages which do not end in divorce. He feels that once an individual has undergone a divorce perhaps he is more likely to engage in another if marital expectations are not being met and thus those remarriages which do not end in divorce have a higher quality of marriage than first marriages. Spanier and Glick (1980) concur.

Problems in Remarriage

Remarriages do face special problems not encountered in first marriages. Cherlin (1978) states that the institution of the family provides no standard solutions to many of the problems of remarriage, with the result that the unity of reconstituted families often becomes precarious. Cherlin (1978) as well as Westoff (1975) and Bernard (1956) stress the importance of language in creating special problems in a marriage. Their basic thesis is that we have not invented a special vocabulary to define the relations among remarried with regard to children, ex-in-laws, and the special familial arrangements of blended families. The point is made that if we do not know what to call what Westoff has referred to as a "cast of thousands" in terms which are not stigmatizing, then how can we expect the blended family to feel assimilated as a familial unit or be readily accepted by main stream society (Price -Bonham, 1980)?

These writers, among others (Duberman, 1976; Rose and Price -Bonham, 1973) form a consensus when discussing problems relating to remarriage. Money, children and the special problems associated with "exs" of all categories present the most pressing problems

11

associated with remarriage.   short, remarriage is
difficult. Generally there are children involved in
the new family unit and while it is difficult enough
for two individuals to establish a relationship alone
it is more than doubly difficult to do so with
additional persons to include in the interaction.
These additional persons in the form of children may
be less than willing participants.

Financial problems stemming from the need to
support newly constituted families while still
contributing to families left behind can create almost
overwhelming economic burdens. Family research has
consistently shown strong correlations between the
amount of money available to a family and the perceived
happiness of that family unit.

Duberman (1976, p. 102) in her study of reconstituted families, after observing several variables such
as education, age, religion, social class and prior
marital status, concludes that "the major reason why
marriages between divorced people tend to be less
successful than those between widowed people is
probably related to this difference in meaning. The
divorced person seeks to escape from an uncomfortable
social position, while the widowed feel no such
necessity." In essence, the negative forces which
push the divorced into remarriages may aid in the
creation of a meaning for marriage which acts to impede
a successful marital relationship.

All contributing problems special to remarriage
could certainly provide ample justification for
termination of a remarriage, however, these factors
alone are not sufficient to explain all multiple
marriages. Too many individuals remain in remarriages
to place the unique problems of remarriage with sole
responsibility for the multi-marrieds. Additional
explanation must be sought.

Identifying the Divorce-Prone

Historically multiple marriers have been viewed
with suspicion and were frequently labeled pathological.
This tendency to see multiple marriers as inadequate
individuals was frequently accompanied by a psycho-
analytic evaluation of their personalities. Individuals who engaged in serial marriage were considered to

be divorce-prone and incapable of sustaining a marital relationship. This assumption implied that these persons would be incapable of marriage no matter what type of social situation or social forces they were exposed to (Cherlin, 1978; Monohan, 1952; Bitterman, 1968). This propensity for labeling multiple marriers as psychologically deficient was so strong that even as insightful a sociologist as Bernard (1956) felt compelled to offer "neuroses" as a weak but possible explanation 24 years ago in her classic <u>Remarriage</u>.

More recently, other researchers have attempted to approach the question of divorce, and therefore, serial marriage and divorce, from a perspective which still attempts to account for the disruption of a marital relationship as a function of inadequate personal skills or impeded personal growth.

Schram (1979) in a study of marital satisfaction, suggests that some unhappy couples may go through a process of dissonance reduction by progressively defining their marriages as happy or acceptable. Given this viewpoint, then it is possible to reverse the reasoning and apply it to multi-marriers. Are multi-marriers individuals who, for whatever reason, have not the ability to engage in dissonance reduction? If dissonance reduction is impossible then perhaps frequent divorce would appear to be the answer for unhappy marriages, however this particular perspective still does not answer why a multi-marrier appears to have difficulty in securing a happy marital relationship.

Berman, Miller, Vines and Lief (1977) assume a developmental approach to the question of divorce and suggest that perhaps individuals are more prone to divorce during specific developmental crises in their lives. They correlate the age 30 crisis with the seven year itch although they do suggest that the boredom in a marital relationship (the honeymoon is over) is more likely to set in after one or two years of marriage. Perhaps multi-marrieds are persons with a low threshold for boredom and seek continual excitement. If we accept this explanation for sequential marriages, then we have returned to seeing serial monogamy as being practiced by inadequate personality types who lack personal commitment and are overly-prone to developmental crises.

13

A number of researchers have suggested that
divorce is accompanied by varying degrees of trauma.
Low trauma is associated with a relatively short
marriage span (Goode, 1956; Smart, 1977). Perhaps
multi-marriers are individuals who experience only
low trauma because they remain in marriages for only
limited periods of time and are never around long
enough to become involved in a relationship to have
the termination of that relationship be traumatic.
Thus, perceptions of the trials and tribulations of
divorcing are not painful and do not operate as a control mechanism.

Today most sociologists have dropped a psycho-
analytic perspective with regard to understanding
divorce and instead have chosen to focus on some
aspect of the individual within a social context.
Many researchers are presently attempting to identify
various social variables which may impact on the
decision to divorce (Bumpass and Sweet, 1972; Gurak
and Dean, 1979; Richardson, 1979; Hays et al, 1980;
Goetting, 1981).

Furstenberg (1979, p. 12) has suggested that
family sociologists "are disinclined to acknowledge
the complexity of our marriage system and continue
to treat divorce and remarriage as departures from
accepted marriage practice" rather than see this
process as possible social change. He argues for the
study of divorce and remarriage as part of a possibly
developing normative schedule that operates to regulate
the flow of individuals in and out of social positions
throughout the life course. This perspective should
encompass both social as well as interpersonal
qualities and therefore provide us with guidelines for
predicting the variables which would act as a catalyst
for the emergence of one phase into another.

Mueller and Pope (1977) believe the tendency to
divorce is transmitted intergenerationally. In other
words, marital instability on the part of the parents
filters down to the children and thus children from
parental marriages that were voluntarily dissolved
will be more likely to dissolve their own marriages
than children from intact parental homes. Some aspect
of social modeling is introduced by this hypothesis.

Spanier and Glick (1980) and Monahan(1959) also
touch on the notion of divorce as a learning process.
Basically stated, they appear to believe that once an

14

individual has undergone one divorce it is much easier
to engage in a second or third. Legal, social and
emotional obstacles have been crossed once so multiple
marriers simply know the routes to take and the consequences of divorce as well as the alternatives.
Implied in this explanation is the incorporation of
social and cultural changes in the form of less stigmatization, easier divorce laws, and more job opportunities for females. This is the most conclusive explanation of how multiple marriers go about the process of
sequential marriages but does not necessarily offer
validation for why any one particular marriage ends in
divorce.

Norton and Glick (1976:18) have stated that "there
appears to be a generally high regard for the ideal of
being married and living as a family member but a
current inability on the part of growing numbers of
couples to achieve and sustain a high level of satisfaction in this sphere without making at least a
second attempt." For some, this attempt to sustain
marital satisfaction may require even three or four
tries. A study of remarriage and redivorce should shed
some insight on why a certain portion of individuals
are not able to successfully maintain a close, harmoni-
ous relationship despite a value system which stresses
marriage.

Furstenburg has additionally suggested that anyone entering marriage is faced with the task of
aligning what in essence can be defined as a "construction of reality" for marriage. "For some, this may
involve a radical revision of self-conception, substantial revision of conjugal roles, and a sharp departure
from the private world view that emerged during the
course of the first (or previous) marriage (1979:16).
Thus, any investigation into the process of multiple
marriage must necessarily involve some study of the
definitions of reality utilized by multiple marriers
as they go about their day- to-day lives.

Research Studies of Multiple Marriage

Despite the rise in theoretical consideration of
divorce-proneness and the process of multiple divorce,
there has been limited research undertaken to support
theorizing. Multiple divorce, or multiple marriage, is
an interesting social phenomenon to ponder but an

extremely difficult one to research. Most of what is known about the multiple married population in the United States is based almost exclusively on a few demographic census and case studies. The focus of attention in multiple marriage has traditionally centered on the act of divorce, as opposed to the act of participating in marriage, and all too frequently those individuals who divorce for the second or third time are categorized as simply "divorced" with no differentiation between those who divorce only once and those who elect divorce more than once.

Monohan (1952) undertook the first attempt to study the multiple divorced population by analyzing census records from 1945 to 1950. His research indicated that the population with three marriages or more accounted for between two and three percent of the marriages in Iowa. He also suggested that divorce following remarriage increased by 10 percent in the five years between 1945 and 1950. Glick and Norton's 1973 demographic study supported Monohan's findings by concluding that over two percent of the male and female population has married for at least three times. However, in 1974 Riley and Spreitzer determined that approximately six percent of both sexes were multiple divorcees.

Bohannan (1970), by case study method, introduced the notion of "divorce chains" and suggested the need for further investigation into the cycle of multiple marriage. Springer, Mangen, and Springer (1975) in their case study of 12 multiple divorcers also alluded to a cycle effect in multiple marriage and suggested various techniques counselors might employ when confronted with clients who possessed a history of multiple divorce.

In brief, these limited studies form the foundation of the investigation into the process of multiple marriage. We know statistically that multiple marriage and divorce exists but unfortunately we know little more than that.

Conclusion

Throughout the course of the literature review this researcher has attempted to present divorce as a dual faceted entity. Divorce can certainly be an

16

answer for an unhappy marital relationship although those seeking release by divorce may be unhappy with the nature of their solution. From a societal perspective this researcher has presented divorce as a solution which is not valued particularly in this society nor is it particularly constrained by various social control mechanisms. Once through a divorce, many individuals will find life quite uncomfortable due to stigmatization, lack of social support, etc., so that they are motivated into seeking another marriage. However, once in that new marriage they may encounter problems due to a lack of total institutionalization of blended families and again be offered with alternatives. The legalities of divorce are much easier to overcome in society today and females are becoming more able to break through prejudice and find occupations which allow for the financial support of families. In short, we value divorce and we do not value divorce. It is seen as an answer to the problem and as the problem itself.

Multi-married individuals can be conceptualized as persons who experience developmental crisis, are less willing to settle or reduce idealism or dissonance, have personality disorders which make them incapable of long-term relationships or as simply people who need constant freedom from boredom. On the other hand, we can also visualize multi-marrieds as persons who learn quickly and learn well. We can see them as being strongly influenced by the amount of divorce they see going on in their environment and through various social processes come to see their own divorce as a viable alternative. Having gone through one divorce and learned the 'ropes' they are much more willing to view another and another divorce as the answer for marital hostility. Multi-marrieds, like divorce, can be conceptualized dichotomously as hero or villian. They are inadequate people in some way who cannot seem to stay married or they are high-minded idealists who simply will not settle for anything but the best.

Why do some people marry frequently? Are multiple marriers somehow different in philosophical orientations, social interactions, tolerance levels than one time marriers? What does "divorce-proneness" imply and how does this category set someone out as being different? What are the social processes involved in multiple marriages? These are but a few of the questions that need to be investigated by research into multiple marriage.

CHAPTER II

METHODOLOGY

Introduction

Marriage, the basic conjugal family form found within the framework of Western society has historically implied a relationship which was characterized by the notion of permanence (Goode, 1962). Within the United States, this idea was seen in the expectation that one lifetime mate would be selected for marriage. While divorce did exist in colonial times, it was a rather minor alteration from the typical family form and was not well tolerated within the community (Gordon, 1978; Seward, 1978). The cultural ideal of one spouse and one marriage was historically given credence by the infrequency of divorce.

Throughout the course of the past 200 years, the United States has experienced a steady rise in rates of divorce, lending validity to the notion that a lifetime commitment to one mate is no longer as culturally ingrained as it once was. In essence, what is implied by the climb in divorce rates is an alteration of the meaning of marriage, at least to the extent that it impacts on mate selection. Thus, as meanings and definitions of social acts which relate directly to the family via marriage become altered by the process of time, the results of these alterations are evidenced in statistical representations of marriage and family life.

However, a true understanding of the alterations within family life requires more than statistical representation. As Rubin (1976) points out:

> We have hundreds of representative studies of one aspect or another of family life-- important and useful studies. We have attitude studies and behavior studies; but few that make the link between the two. We have probability statistics on marriage, divorce, sexual behavior, and much, much more; but they tell us nothing of the experience of the flesh-and-blood women and men who make up the numbers. This is not a failure of those studies; they are not designed to do so. Still, they leave us with only a fragment of knowledge. There-

18

fore, we need also social science that is
so designed-qualitative studies that can
capture the fullness of experience, the
richness of living. We need work that
takes us inside the family dynamics, into
the socio-emotional world in which people
are born, live, and die--real people with
flesh, blood, bones, and skeletons (p.13).

To understand fully marriage and family life
within an experiential context, research efforts
must be geared towards the ground floor, to an understanding of the ways in which individuals participating
in the idea of family utilize their notions of family
life for making sense out of their world. This research effort is an attempt to come to some understanding of a social phenomenon which has been measured
by social demographers, lamented by social philosophers
criticized by theologians, but left relatively un-
researched by social scientists.

This investigation into the process of multiple
marriage uses a qualitative approach in an attempt to
give insight and create additional knowledge of one
aspect of family life which has successfully been
charted statistically but which yields only frag-
mentary understanding of the socio-emotional world
in which multi-marriers are born, live and die. This
research effort is an attempt to elaborate on a
statistical fact and create for the reader an understanding of the real people who comprise the social
category of multiple marrier.

A Methodological Approach to Researching

Multiple Marriages

Statistics have indicated that for a small, but
rising, number of persons in this society, the
establishment of a successful marriage is problematic.
The past two decades have seen not only an increase
in the tendency on the part of people to divorce, but
also an inclination on the part of some to divorce and
remarry more than once. This marital history has
been referred to at various times as serial marriage,
serial polygyny, or multiple marriage. In essence,
what is occuring is the formation of a new pattern of
activity which revolves around the concept of marriage
and gives rise to the notion that, for those individuals who choose to participate in multiple marriage,

the more traditional definitions, expectations, and meanings usually associated with marriage have somehow been altered.

At the present time we have sufficient demographic information to illustrate the existence of a small group of individuals who engage in the practice of multiple marriage. However, what is lacking in research concerning multiple marriage is an understanding of why this occurs and insight into exactly how the individual goes about engaging in this process. To have a true understanding of the why and how of multiple marriage, it is necessary to enter into the social world of the multiple marrier and seek answers to our questions from those who know it best, the multiple marriers.

Lofland (1971) has pointed out that to have any real understanding of the behavior patterns expressed by any specific group, it is necessary to conduct an analysis from the standpoint of that group.

> A first step is to recognize that any
> participants under study are themselves
> analytic. They order and pattern their
> views and their activities. While their
> world may seem random and chaotic to an
> outsider, it is a safe bet it is not that
> way to insiders . . . It becomes possible
> for (the researcher) to provide a more
> articulate and clearer protrayal of that
> order than the participants are likely to
> work up. The analyst seeks to provide an
> explicit rendering of the structure, order,
> and patterns found among a set of partici-
> pants (p. 7).

This research into the process of multiple marriage is an attempt to ascertain the how and why of multiple marriage as a process, to gain intuitive understanding of the social nature of the world as seen from the viewpoint of those who know it best. It is an attempt to provide a rendering of the structure, order and patterns found among multi-marriers. Lofland (1971) has also noted that:

> to live in the modern world is to know about
> very many more categories of human beings
> than one knows directly. That simple fact
> sets up a fundamental dynamic in the experi-
> ence of modern people. To begin to know of

a category of person is to begin to build
a fuller portrait of them. To have a label
that specifies the existence of a set of
persons is to begin to conceive of what
'those people' are like (p. 1).

While it is true that readers of this work cannot
have the face-to-face experience of actually coming
to know multi-marriers in a personal sense, it is
hoped that this research will help to break down the
barriers which leave the multi-marriers, for the most
part, "known about" rather than "known".

In order to bridge the gap between the "known
about" and the "known", to create understanding of
the process of multiple marriage as it is engaged in
by those individuals who are categorized as multi-
marriers, it is essential to utilize a methodology
which is designed to capture the process as on-going
human activity. Multiple marriage exists as a form
of reality for those participants, and as Blumer
(1969, p. 22) explains,"The world of reality exists
only in human experience and only in the form in
which humans 'see' that world." A methodology to
investigate multiple marriage then, must necessarily
present a "world of reality" from the perspective of
the multi-marrier.

Many social scientists view human behavior as
a product of how people interpret their world.

The task of the methodologist is to capture
this process of interpretation. To do this
requires what Weber called verstehen, empathic
understanding or an ability to reproduce in
one's own mind the feelings, motives, and
thoughts behind the actions of others (Bogden
and Taylor, 1975, p. 14).

Thus, in order to understand multiple marriage as a
process, the most direct route, and the only true
route, is one which involves an interaction with those
who engage in the process and by doing so, allows
those individuals to articulate their "world of
reality" as they see it and live it.

The research problem guiding this investigation
into the process of multiple marriage is then a
methodological question of how best to grasp understanding of human activity. The approach utilized to

21

gain insight is based on the assumption that in order
to understand the interpretations of a specific category of people, one is directed to those individuals
who compose that category and initial understanding
comes only from the study of the spoken words and
observable acts of the participants. Utilizing a
qualitative methodology, this study then, is an
exploratory study of the world of the multi-marrier.

The Methodology Employed

Bogdan and Taylor (1975, p. 4) have defined
qualitative methodologies as "referring to research
procedures which produce descriptive data: people's
own written or spoken words and observable behavior",
in essence, "material in which people reveal in their
own words their view of their entire life or part of
it, or some other aspect about themselves".

The descriptive data gathered for this research
project consists of three types of personal documenta-
tion. The first of these, in-depth interviews, forms
the foundation of the material under analysis, while
two additional sources, personal letters and one
diary, compliment and add clarity to the information
obtained by interview. The research methodology is
presented in three parts; selection of the respondents,
collection of descriptive data, and analysis of this
data.

Selecting the Sample

A multi-marrier, for purposes of qualifying for
participation in this research project, was defined
as any individual who possessed a marital history of
at least two legal marriages and subsequent divorces.
Inasmuch as the process of mate selection appeared to
potentially be an important element in the process of
multiple marriage, those individuals who were presently
divorced from second spouses and identified themselves
as dating, and therefore had established for themselves a conceptual pool of eligibles, fulfilled the
minimal requirement for participation in the research.

While divorces are a matter of public record and,
as such, are published in the newspaper as well as
being recorded in county and state records, there is
no available source which readily identifies individuals who have engaged in multiple marriages. This
type of information is quite private and difficult to
obtain. In order to obtain a sample of respondents

for participation in this research, it was necessary to approach initially individuals who might have access to this type of information. Ministers, counselors, educators and social workers were approached and asked for any possible referrals of multi-marriers. On the basis of the referrals obtained from these professionals, approximately half of the respondents were secured.

In securing the remaining portion of respondents utilized in this research, a sampling technique known as the snowball sample was employed. Babbie (1979) refers to this technique as a nonprobability sampling method which involves asking each person interviewed to suggest additional people for interviewing. As Goffman (1963) has noted, often individuals who share a common attribute are aware of others in the same category. In the case of the multi-marrier, this proved to be a valid observation and the remaining respondents were secured on the basis of referrals by multi-marriers already interviewed. A total of twenty multi-marriers were approached for possible inclusion in the research project with only two refusing to participate.

All respondents were told that this research was undertaken in an attempt to come to some understanding about marriage in general and those individuals who marry more than twice specifically. All individuals interviewed were interested in the project and responded to all questions with a great deal of candor. Assurances of anonymity were given to all respondents and most of the respondents requested copies of this study at its conclusion.

The Interview and Other Personal Documentation

After making contact with a respondent, either through a professional or by snowball sample, an appointment was set up at the convenience of the respondent. It was explained to the respondent that the work would consist of an intensive interview at which time the respondent would be asked to present a biographical history of his life, with particular emphasis on the recounting of marriages and divorces.

All interviews, with the exception of one which took place in this researcher's office, occurred in the homes of the respondents. The interviews lasted between three and six hours. Those interviews lasting over three hours were conducted in two sessions. All interviews, with the exception of one, were tape recorded and later transcribed on to paper. Generally, only the respondent and this researcher were present throughout entire course of the interview. On occasion children of the respondent being interviewed were present in the home and this necessitated various interruptions for bathroom and water breaks. On four occasions I was introduced to the respective spouse or roommate of the interviewee prior to being left alone with the respondent for the interview. Interviews were occasionally conducted while the respondent engaged in household tasks, such as washing or ironing. While this type of interviewing proved to be difficult at times due to constant interruptions, overall, it worked to create an environment in which the respondent felt at home and as a result, unusually thoughtful responses were elicited.

The basic format of the interview itself consisted of a series of open-ended questions designed to elicit information concerning family background, marital history, value and belief systems, mate selection patterns, and conceptualizations of marriage as a personal experience. Interviewees were asked to be as specific as possible in terms of reconstructing personal responses to each succeeding marriage and divorce in an attempt to ascertain changes in perceptions of self and marriage over time. Respondents were encouraged to elaborate on any particular aspect of the questioning that they felt was relevant to their own biography. Due to the intimate nature of the interview, the interaction which occured during the interview was often emotionally upsetting for the respondent and frequently the role of the researcher was altered to also include that of being a non-judgmental listener.

In addition to transcribed interviews, two other types of personal documents were made available to the researcher by respondents during the course of the interviews. Two female respondents turned to personal letters which they had saved over the years for clarification of certain historical points and allowed the researcher to read them also. One female respondent frequently referred to her diary, a journal which she had kept through the course of two of her three marriages, and gave permission for the reproduction of any portions of the diary. Excerpts of this diary are used extensively throughout Chapter III.

24

Description of the Respondents

Since this research is a presentation of the social world of a particular category of persons, multi-marriers, and utilizes as a basis for understanding this social phenomenon their perceptions of the process of multiple marriage, it is necessary to have some knowledge of the individuals who joined together to create this special social grouping. While it is not unique aspects of each individual's biography which is of interest in defining a commonality of experience, an overall view of social attributes which these individuals share singularly and in common aid in giving substance to an enlarged perspective.

In all, ten women and eight men participated in this research. The ages of the respondents ranged from 26 to 39 and included a marital history of between two to six marriages and divorces. A summary of demographic information, in terms of social class and family background is presented in Table I. As the reader may note, there are certain similarities relating to social class and family background which appear to be relevant in a definitional composition of multi-marriers. These shared attributes are considered to have an effect on the process of multi-marriage and will be discussed in the text of this research report. The assigning of social class standing for the respondents was based on a self-assessment on the part of the participants as well as an objective evaluation by the researcher.

Again, in terms of presenting a summary of information, Table II also indicates a similarity of pattern with regard to the timing of various marriages and divorces. Since time is considered to be an essential element in the understanding of this social phenomenon, it also will be discussed in the text.

The Analysis

At the completion of the interviews, an analysis of the material was undertaken in order to observe any generic responses among the self-reporting of the participants. A commonality of experience, both in terms of actual marital history and the perceptions, meanings, and definitions derived from such a biography, were assumed to indicate shared elements which compose the process of multiple marriage. For clarity

25

TABLE I

RESPONDENTS' DEMOGRAPHIC INFORMATION IN TERMS OF
SOCIAL CLASS AND FAMILY BACKGROUND

Name	Age	Educational Level	Present SES	Present Occupation	Family Background as a Child	Present Living Arrangement
Jeff	37	Some College	Middle	Lt. in fire department	Born 2nd of two sons to career military father, housewife mother. Father enlisted soldier. Family status: Lower-middle class.	Respondent lives with third wife. One son, by second marriage who lives with mother; rates present marriage as stable.
Will	30	High School Graduate	Lower Middle	Auto Mechanic	Born 3rd son to family of eight children, father fundamentalist minister; mother housewife. Family status: Lower middle class.	Lives alone in an apartment; has one son who he has not seen in over six years.
Fred	37	Some College	Middle	Police Officer	Oldest of three sons to military father & housewife mother. Father enlisted career military. Family status: Lower middle class.	Presently lives with fiancee; plans to remarry shortly; has one daughter who lives with 1st wife; rates present relationship as stable.

TABLE I (Continued)

Name	Age	Educational Level	Present SES	Present Occupation	Family Background as a Child	Present Living Arrangement
Patty	30	2nd year of College	Lower	Student	Born 2nd of 2 daughters & 2 sons. Father truck driver, mother housewife. Parents divorced at early age & remarried when respondent was five. Father alcoholic. Family status: Lower middle class.	Lives with third, student husband; has 3 children by previous marriages, is pregnant by present husband. Rates present marriage as good but unstable.
Lisa	32	Medical Doctor	Upper Middle	In private Practice	Oldest of 3 daughters; father oilfield employee, mother housewife; parents divorced when respondent was 18. Family status: Middle class.	Lives with only child in surburban home; presently dating one man but has no plans to remarry at this time.
David	30	2 years College	Lower Middle	Rock Musician	Born eldest of 3 sons to middle managment, father & housewife mother. Father died when respondent was 19. Family status: Middle class.	Lives with brother in urban apartment at present, is dating no particular person, but eventually desires remarriage.

TABLE I (Continued)

Name	Age	Educational Level	Present SES	Present Occupation	Family Background as a Child	Present Living Arrangement
Mark	36	2 years College	Upper Middle	Vice-Pres Insurance Company	Born to upper middle middle class family One younger brother & sister, father radio executive, mother housewife. Family status: Middle class.	Lives alone in suburban home at present time, is not dating anyone. Father of 2 daughters by 1st two wives, desires remarriage.
Sheila	29	H.S. G.E.D. Some College	Lower Middle	Telephone Lineman	Born middle child of five siblings to frequently divorced alcoholic mother. Respondent raised in extreme poverty.	Lives with son in apartment, is presently dating someone & hopes to remarry soon.
Angela	33	H.S.	Middle	Housewife Secretary	Born eldest of 2 daughters & 2 sons to lower class family, father truck driver, mother housewife. Family status: Lower Middle.	Presently lives in urban home with daughter by 1st marriage & 3rd husband; rates present marriage as good but probably unstable.

28

TABLE I (Continued)

Name	Age	Educational Level	Present SES	Present Occupation	Family Background as a Child	Present Living Arrangement
Frieda	35	M.S. Degree	Upper Middle	Child Abuse Case Worker	Only child of older parents, father oil-field roughneck, mother housewife. Father frequently unemployed. Family status: Lower class.	Lives in suburban home with two sons by previous husbands; is present-ly involved with divorced man and is contemplating remarriage.
Lois	27	M.S. Degree	Middle	School Teacher	Oldest of 2 daughters, mother divorced 3 times while respondent in family home. Family status: Lower class.	Lives in urban home with only child by last husband, is not dating at this time but desires to remarry eventu-ally.
Martha	26	3 years College	Lower Middle	Student	Born to large Catholic family of 3 daughters & 2 sons, father died at 14, mother remarried 5 years later. Family status: Lower Middle class.	Presently lives alone in apartment, no children, is dating one man but no plans for marriage at this time.

TABLE I (Continued)

Name	Age	Educational Level	Present SES	Present Occupation	Family Background as a Child	Present Living Arrangement
John	39	High School	Lower Middle	Auto Mechanic	Born only child to janitor father & housewife mother, 4 half siblings from father's previous marriage. Family status: Lower class.	Presently lives alone in trailer house, has no interaction with 3 daughters by previous marriages, hopes to eventually marry but dates no one at this time.
Charles	41	Ph.D.	Upper Middle	College Professor	Oldest son of lower class family, one brother & sister, father truck driver mother housewife. Family status: Lower middle	Lives in suburban home with 3rd wife, has 3 daughters by previous marriages who he sees infrequently, rates present marriage as good but unstable.
Janis	35	Vocational Nurse LPN	Lower Middle	Staff Nurse Hospital	Born the older of 2 daughters to salesman father & housewife mother, parents divorced while respondent was still	Lives in rural home with only child by 2nd marriage and third husband; rates present marriage

TABLE I (Continued)

Name	Age	Educational Level	Present SES	Present Occupation	Family Background as a Child	Present Living Arrangement
					in family home. Family status: Middle class.	as stable.
Jean	27	High School	Lower Middle	Telephone Repairman	Mother divorced prior to birth, 1 older sister, raised in grandparents home, farming family. Mother remarried. Family status: Lower middle class.	Lives in trailer house with live-in boyfriend, no children, desires to remarry but not to present roommate.
Meg	39	M.S. Degree	Lower Middle	Student	Oldest of 2 brothers & 2 sisters, father died at early age, mother institutionalized, raised by lower income aunt. Family Status: Lower middle class.	Lives alone in apartment; only child, a daughter, lives with father no contact with child in over 8 years; is not dating at present time but desires eventual remarriage.

TABLE I (Continued)

Name	Age	Educational Level	Present SES	Present Occupation	Family Background as a Child	Present Living Arrangement
Tom	39	College Graduate	Lower Middle	Postal Worker	Born oldest of 2 sons to Canadian railroad worker father & housewife mother. Family status: Lower class.	Lives alone in urban apartment, has one son by 1st wife whom he has not seen in 8 years, dates no one at present time but anticipates remarriage.

TABLE II

RESPONDENTS' LENGTH OF MARRIAGES AND TIMES SINGLE

Name	Age at First Marriage	Length of 1st Marriage	Length of Time Single	Length of 2nd Marriage	Length of Time Single	Length of 3rd Marriage	Length of Time Single	Length of 4th Marriage	Length of Time Single	Length of 5th Marriage	Length of Time Single
Jeff	18	3 yrs	1 yr	2½ yrs	3 yrs	3 yrs*					
Will	17	1½ yrs	3 days	1½ yrs	10 mos	3 yrs	3 yrs	1 mo	9 mos	5 mos	2 mos*
Fred	20	10 yrs	7 mos	2 mos	1 yr	2 yrs	7 mos	2 mos	2 yrs*		
Patty	16	3 yrs	1 yr	2 mos	6 yrs	1 yr*					
Lisa	24	3 yrs	1½ yrs	2 yrs	9 mos*						
David	19	6 mos	10 mos	2 mos	8 yrs*						
Mark	22	2 yrs	3 yrs	8 yrs	1 mo	2 mos*					
Sheila	16	5 yrs	2 yrs	2 yrs	2 yrs	2 mos*					
Angela	19	5 mos	1 yr	4 yrs	7 yrs	2 mos*					
Frieda	20	10 mos	1 yr	6 yrs	2 yrs	4 mos	3 mos*				
Lois	18	2 yrs	1 yr / 6 mos	3 mos	2 yrs	5 yrs	6 mos*				
Martha	21	9 mos	4 mos	9 mos	2 yrs*						
John	17	5 yrs	6 mos	4 yrs	3 yrs	1 yr / 2 mos	2 mos	3½yrs	2 yrs	6 mos	2 mos
Charles	20	8 yrs	6 mos	8 yrs	6 mos	2 yrs*					
Janis	17	4½ yrs	4 mos	3 yrs	3 mos	5 yrs					
Jean	18	3 yrs	9 mos	10 mos	2 yrs*						
Meg	16	2 yrs	3 yrs	2 yrs	1½ yrs	6 mos	2 mos	1 mo	2 yrs	2 mos	1 yr*
Tom	19	6 yrs	6 mos	6 mos	6 yrs*	5 yrs	6 mos*				

*at time of interview

33

of purpose in reporting the data, direct quotations from particular respondents are frequently offered to the reader. These quotes are judged to be most representative of all the responses elicited in discussions of specific points.

The remaining chapters of this work present an assessment of the process of multiple marriage, as it has been experienced and is articulated by those who know it best, the multi-marriers. It is a way of seeing, describing, and explaining this process of sequential marriage by presenting the perceptions of those who participate in it. This researcher realizes, that for some researchers, the methodology used for drawing the sample and analyzing the data is open to criticism. However, in anticipation of such criticism, this researcher offers Rubin's (1976) appraisal of this type of methodology:

> I am aware that both the methods of this study and the style of presentation are vulnerable to criticism from colleagues in the social science. The small sample not randomly chosen makes generalizations suspect. The anecdotal presentation raises the question of representativeness in the use of data. The only answer to these criticisms lies in the quality of work itself--in its ability to persuade by appealing to a level of 'knowing' that exists in all of us but is not very often tapped; in its ability to borrow a phase from psychology--to generate an 'aha experience' (p. 5).

The analysis presented in this work is intended to be suggestive, not directive, and hopes to create an awareness on the part of the reader rather than formulate a definitive statement on multiple marriage.

CHAPTER III

THE EARLY YEARS

The Importance of Childhood

During the course of describing the social world of any specific category of persons it is often necessary to allow history, in terms of personal biography, to initiate the telling. As Mills (1959, p. 6) explains, "No social study that does not come back to the problems of biography, of history and of their intersection within a society has completed its intellectual journey". A complete understanding of the careers engaged in by "multiple marriers" and the processes involved in the acting out of such life-styles must begin where the lives of these individuals merge with on-going society. We begin our journey into the social world of the multiple marrier with an exploration of the childhoods of this category of persons.

As social scientists we are often interested in the socialization processes in childhood because we are aware that frequently people within a given society have shared experiences which aid them in defining their social world. In this sense, multiple marriers share commonalities of childhood experiences which aid in fashioning perceptions of social life.

There is a real danger in presenting information on childhood socialization and experiences. All too often it is assumed that this type of information implies a causative variable which constrains the individual throughout the course of a lifetime. Reciting early childhood experiences within a family context is utilized in this study to represent the family unit as an agent of socialization and as a primary group. In this sense, we employ the family unit of multiple marriers as a "Meadian Construct" with the understanding that each person approaches his world from the standpoint of the culture of his group (Berger and Berger, 1979).

As has been pointed out countless times, the child grows in a family setting by sharing certain assumptions and experiences with other family members. For this reason, in terms of understanding the importance the family plays in the life of the multiple marrier, we need to be aware of the significance of those "initial others" in aiding to fashion the manner in which the young perceives his social world. As Berger and Berger (1964) explain,

> Only by internalizing the voices of others can we speak to ourselves. If no one had significantly addressed us from the outside, there would be silence within ourselves as well. It is only through others that we can come to discover ourselves. This, among other reasons, is why it is so important to choose one's parents with some care (p. 14).

While it is true that the family represents for the young child his first experience with a social world and it often happens that family members become generalized others, this specific point should not be construed as totally directive nor completely explanatory. We need to be cognizant of the fact that internalization of norms, values and belief systems occur which are often in direct opposition to those which the family may advocate (Shibutani, 1955).

> First of all in modern societies special problems arise from the fact that men sometimes use standards of groups in which they are not recognized members, sometimes of groups that do not exist at all. Second, in our mass society, characterized as it is by cultural pluralism, each person internalizes several perspectives, and this occasionally gives rise to embarrassing dilemmas which call for systematic study (p. 564).

Through the course of this chapter we will point out ways in which the socializing family appears to greatly influence the early perceptions of the multi-marrier while at the same time alluding to courses of action which clearly demonstrate opposition to that which one would naturally assume to occur given the familial background. This first chapter attempts to show to what extent those "voices from the outside", whether they originate from family members or persons outside the family context, initiate the creation of lifestyle choices. In giving the historical biography of these individuals it is hoped that the reader may glimpse the ways in which early constructions of realities are generated.

There are several major themes to be aware of

which emerge during this chapter. There appears to
be a less than subtle adherence to sex roles incul-
cated into the young multi-marrier as he grows. We
begin to see a clear dedication to concepts of
masculinity and feminity. Early in the life of the
multiple marrier we see an orientation on the part
of young males to a social world which exists outside the family unit. For females, we see a strong
turning inward, to family, and to expectations of the
roles women should play in a male-dominated society.
These internalized sex role orientations, on the part
of both males and females, eventually influence
decisions to leave the family home and marry.

During these early years of socialization
fledgling concepts of social identities are formed.
The intertwining of family relationships, hardships,
and the emergence into a society at large which exists
outside the family unit join together to create the
basis of "self" for the young multi-marrier. During
the childhood years experienced by the multi-marrier
we begin to have some understanding of the needs,
desires, and expectations of the child as he attempts
to fashion for himself an identity which is more or
less satisfying as he matures into adulthood.

This first chapter is an attempt to tell a story.
It is a story composed of social meanings, of
definitions and vocabulary of motives within an
historical framework. It is an attempt to build an
understanding of the perceptions of a category of
persons as they engage in a portion of their life
experience.

The Childhood Home: Early Encounters

With a Social World

I can remember being five years old and
sitting on the porch steps watching other
little children being called into supper
and wishing I was one of them. It didn't
seem fair. They were so happy and I was so
unhappy.
                                        -Frieda

For most multi-marriers, growing up does not
represent a time of happy family relationships,
picnics in the park or bright pink birthday parties.
Instead, each recollection of childhood brings with

it a wave of insecurity and, for the most part, a memory composed of distaste and threads of ugliness. Nostalgia is not evidenced as these individuals reflect back on disrupted family unity, financial struggles and years of personal and emotional hardship.

The early years were often spent in homes where happiness and security were fleeting episodes caught within a web of confusion and turmoil. Most recall their childhood in terms of bitter lessons learned and, for a surprising number, in terms of the number of scars and bruises received from angry parents. Of all the people talked with, only three could state that theirs had been a happy childhood. For the rest, tales of childhood homes centered on the inter-relationship of poverty, frequent moves, an astonishing number of step-parents, and poor family relations. These stories combined to create what most Americans would consider a very dismal history.

The majority of the homes and family relationships described here are similar to the families written about by others. These are the homes of the working class and lower middle class families explored by Komarovsky (1962) and Rubin (1976). There are some differences between the homes of the multi-marriers and those homes visited by Rubin and perhaps it is these differences which nurture an environment for the multi-marrier. Unlike the respondents in Rubin's work, these individuals, the multiple marriers, are acutely aware of the pain generated from a troublesome family.

The homes which reared multi-marriers were, in the perceptions of the respondents, fragmented homes which lacked a firm foundation of love and security. Lack of money and overcrowdedness were primary con-cerns. The stability of the family was often dis-rupted by the departure of family members and there were seldom any persons outside the family with whom close relationships could be formed.

On the whole, for these families, there appeared to be few ties with community groups or organizations. The parents of the multi-marriers did not belong to any formal clubs and seldom even joined loose social gatherings. Education was not highly valued and children were seldom encouraged to seek a different or better lifestyle. The only major tie to any type of organization found outside the family was the church.

In approximately half of the families some form of
church affiliation was encouraged. The churches
chosen by the parents were generally fundamental
organizations which advocated a strict biblical
interpretation and code of personal conduct. For the
adolescent multi-marrier being influenced by a more
liberal attitude from society at large, this one strong
tie to a group outside the family often became
problematic.

With allegiance to outside organizations being
discouraged, multi-marriers as young children were
primarily influenced by the family unit. The growth
of these children in these homes, and the recollection
of childhood relationships produce some insight into
the eventual lifestyles chosen by multi-marriers.

Unhappy Homes: The Initial Meaning of Family

The early years were hard ones, a time most
multi-marriers later spent in attempting to overcome
in a variety of strategies.

> I guess you could say I was relatively
> happy as a child. Most of what I remember
> of my childhood is a lot of noise, people
> yelling at each other. I swore when I grew
> up I wouldn't have so much noise all the
> time and now I don't.
> >   -David, age 30, divorced twice.

This statement is from a young man who is twice
divorced, with each divorce being preceeded by a
demand on his wife's part to begin a family. Other
multi-marriers began an attempt to achieve a sense of
normalacy very early in their lives.

> I was always unhappy as a child and I was
> always looking for happiness. It was a
> continual search. I made friends only with
> those kids who has a normal home so I could
> be in those houses a lot. I used to pretend
> they were my home. I was very social as a
> child and would be so friendly the parents
> would like me around. When a girlfriend
> of mine had parents who got divorced, I
> dropped her as a friend. Her home wasn't
> normal anymore.
> >   Lois, age 27, divorced 3 times.

Another young woman, divorced three times, describes
her present lifestyle in terms of her guilt over a
childhood of poverty.

> My mother used to tell me that she was so
> happy when I was born but I never believed
> her. When I was growing up we were always
> poor. There was never enough money. Mom
> had a scrapbook of pictures of she and Dad
> of the time before I was born. They had
> new cars and big houses then. I guess all
> that changed after I was born. I decided
> when I was little that no one would have
> to suffer on my account again. If there
> isn't enough money, I get out (of relation-
> ships and marriages).
>
> > -Frieda, age 35.

Alcohol played a large part in the creation of
painful memories. Almost half of the people interviewed credited alcoholic parents with being the
motivating factor in unpleasantness.

> My father was a drinker and when he had
> been out drinking he would come home in
> the middle of the night and get us kids
> up out of bed and yell at us or hit on us.
> The next morning he wouldn't even remember
> it.
>
> > -Angela, age 33, married 3 times.

> Home to me was a place to stay away from.
> My father was an alcoholic but he finally
> left when I was eight. Of course, by then
> Mom was drinking too. Mom married three
> more times before I finally left home but
> she never stayed married long. She was
> kind of hard to get along with.
>
> > -Sheila, age 27, divorced 3 times.

> There wasn't much to being at home. It
> was all right. Of course, Dad was a
> trucker then and when he had had a few
> belts the fur would fly. I never got
> hit by him because I could tell when he
> came home drinking and I got scarce until
> he was sober.
>
> > -Charles, age 41, 3rd marriage.

For a few respondents, particularly males,

40

unpleasant memories are tenuously hidden under a veil
of nostalgia which is rapidly ripped away in reflection. One man, divorced five times, tells of the
happy times associated with his childhood in a
family of eight children.

>It was nice being raised with that many
>brothers and sisters. We were kind of a
>Walton type family.
>>-Will, age 30, divorced 5 times.

"Because of that nice memory of a large family did
you also want to have a large family?"

>Good Lord, no! I only have one child from
>my first marriage and he was an accident.
>I don't want any children. They are too
>much trouble and all that confusion. I
>guess . . . I guess we weren't much of a
>Walton family after all.

    Interestingly, female multi-marriers readily
acknowledge their early years as a period of unhappiness and powerful loneliness while males appear to
initially present their boyhoods as relatively carefree, only to allow contradictory glimpses of unhappiness to occasionally slip out. A police officer,
Fred, age 37, divorced from his fourth wife, described
his early years as "typical of everyone else's". Much
later in the interview he began to discuss his views
on child rearing.

>I think a child needs a certain amount of
>discipline. I was disciplined as a child
>regularly by my father.

"How did he discipline you?"

>Oh, he used to beat me with a stick he kept
>behind the kitchen door. I guess today he
>would have been tried for child abuse but
>back then no one said anything no matter
>how many bruises a kid got.

"Do you agree with your father's form of discipline
for your own children?"

>Hell, no! I have arrested people for doing
>the same thing.

Another man, presently in his third marriage, describes his childhood as stable and happy only later to elaborate on the early years with a certain amount of remorse. "What kind of relationship do you have with your daughters?'

> Not nearly as close as I would like, although I don't really want to see them anymore than I do. When I was growing up I was totally indifferent to my family. My home was just somewhere I happened to sleep and sometimes eat. My family didn't know who I was or what I did. I came and went at will and now it is hard to remember any of my childhood in relationship to my family. What I do remember centers around me and only very peripherally with my family. I hope my daughters don't recall their childhood like I do.
> -Charles, 41, presently in 3rd marriage.

While discussing childhood experiences with multi-marriers one is rapidly struck by the dicotomous memories of early childhood. Why are females so much quicker to label a childhood as unhappy while males seem reluctant or refuse to do so? Surely being beaten by a father or living in a home where other family members are only peripherally involved with one's life is as traumatic in its own way as those family homes experienced by females?

The Rise of Masculinity and Femininity

As interviews progressed many differences were noted with regard to male and female perceptions of social life. Those elements in a female's life which reach paramount importance are perceived as grossly diminished in scale by males. Bernard (1972), Rubin (1976) and others have written much on this phenomonen, this differential process of socialization of males and females. Both authors suggest females are socialized early to describe their lives in terms of their relationships with others, in this case, family members. Relationships define for the female her quality of life. Of course, if she perceived her family life as bad, the memories are so much stronger and prevalent in adulthood. Men, whose lives are centered on achievements and not relationships, are not condemned to define themselves or their past histories in terms of others. While alcoholic fathers, beatings, and other family members can be seen as only peripheral to the biography

of a man's life, they are the critical core of the
woman's. This same phenomenon, slightly altered in
form, occurs over and over throughout the life course
of multi-marriers. Unhappy childhood homes, experienced by males and females alike, are processed
differently and have varying prominence in adulthood.
Females readily describe unhappiness as children, men,
more slowly, and with only gradual lifting of the veil
which obscures the vision of unpleasantness.

As previously noted, in reflecting on childhood
memories, we begin to initially observe a varying in
the perceptions of males and females. The emergence
of sex role orientations can account for the discrep-
ancies in recollections. As young girls, female
multi-marriers have been socialized into concentrating
on relational elements in their lives while young men
have been directed away from such constraints. The
basic differences between the sex role orientations
evidenced here is simply described as the difference
between 'doing' and 'being' (Chodorow, 1971). Young
male multi-marriers are early in life taught that in
order to receive validation of self it is essential
to achieve, to engage in the active <u>doing</u> of some
specific task. Female multi-marriers, as young girls,
have been shown that validation is given for simply
being a particular type of person. Little girls can
simply be a nice girl or be a pretty girl and not
necessarily have to be actively engaged in doing anything. Little boys, by virtue of being male, quickly
learn that climbing the highest tree or scoring a
home run is the easiest avenue for achieving the
validation given to girls for simply existing as
females.

Thus we see a concentration on the part of
female multi-marriers to being involved in a relationship with parents and siblings, and later husbands
and lovers. Validation of self is achieved by engaging
in relationships with others, by 'being' the counter-
part of a dyad or a group. For male multi-marriers,
being involved in a relationship is not seen as an
active orientation. One must go out and 'do' something, not simply 'be' something. Given the orientation of the two sexes to the differences between
being and doing, there is little question as to why
female multi-marriers are so much more acutely aware,
have so much more vivid memories of the relationships
experienced within the family home.

43

<u>Living Through It: Alienation from the</u>

<u>Concept of Family</u>

     For many multi-marriers growing up was a process
they conceptualize as something to be 'lived through'
in order to get it over with, much as most Americans
live through income tax or costly automobile repairs.
Much of the unhappiness attributed to childhood stems
from an early feeling of alienation from family, often
at times appearing self-imposed.

> I always felt different from the rest of
> my family. I never felt like I was really
> one of them. I never wanted to be one of
> them.
>   -Lois, age 27, divorced 3 times.

> Somehow it just seemed that I turned out
> to have nothing in common with my sisters.
> We were not alike.
>   -Jean, age 27, divorced 2 times.

> I never felt like I really belonged. Every-
> one else liked my step-father but I didn't.
> When I was older I talked with my mother
> about how I didn't feel like I was really
> accepted by the rest of them. She told me
> that wasn't so. However, when I turned
> eighteen and first left home, one weekend
> I went home to visit and they had moved to
> another town and hadn't told me. I went
> home and no one lived there anymore. That's
> how much of a part of the family I was.
>   -Martha, age 26, divorced 2 times.

"Did you not know they were planning on moving?"

     Yes, they told me they were moving but not when.
Becoming alienated from the rest of the family appears
to be one way of separating oneself from the trauma of
pain and confusion. If only one can learn to care
not so much, then the pain of violence and lack of
love is diminished.

> Sure, I had a hard life. I had to live
> through a lot. But I did it. I just
> stayed away from home until way past dark
> and only went home to sleep.
>   -Angela, 33, 3rd marriage.

When I was growing up I spent as much time
away from home as possible. I would spend
the nights with my aunt and grandmother.
Sometimes I would stay with my girlfriend.
If I had to sleep at home only two nights
out of the week I would count myself lucky.
                    -Patty, age 30, 3rd marriage.

One time I got an award at school and didn't
tell my mother I was getting it. She found
out about it later and asked me why I
hadn't told her. I didn't want her to come
to school to see me get it. I wanted my
own life.
                    -Lois, age 27, divorced 3 times.

Separating oneself from the people who are
responsible for unhappiness is a lesson multi-marriers
appear to learn at an early age. Young boys, given
more freedom in youth due to their sex, utilized this
procedure more frequently than did their female
counterparts. At a later point in this study, we
shall see that this means of avoiding unpleasant
interactions also applies to marriages.

Family Relationships: Interactions with

Early "Significant Others"

For the multi-marrier, home is not where the
heart is and is remembered as a place from which most
urgently wished for an early departure. Many placed
blame for early disenchantments on the inability of
parents to maintain a solid home, free from anger and
hostility openly expressed to each other.

A Biblical scripture notes that the sins of the
father are not visited upon the child but in the case
of the multi-marrier, it is often the perceived sins
of the parents which generate a unifying threat from
one generation to the next. The recalled unhappiness
and problems of childhood related by the respondents
suggest, that for many, parental memories provoke
recollections of episodes of behavior which at times
stand both as a model for living and as a negative
example. Most commented that the pain of childhood
stemmed in some manner from the inability of parents
to provide a sheltered and secure environment.
Accusations of irresponsiblity and lack of love still
have the ability to bring tears or grimaces of anger

45

although the individual may well have not lived in the parental home for over twenty years.

> People like that shouldn't be allowed to
> bring children into the world. No kid
> should have to go through what I did.
>   -Janis, age 33, 3rd marriage.

> One time my sister was going to report my
> father to the police for beating us but
> they wouldn't accept her word. Mom had to
> back her up and she wouldn't do it. How
> can any mother just let that happen to her
> children? I still don't understand why
> she just let him do that to us. Today I am
> scared that I might start to abuse my
> children also. I haven't and I don't want
> to but look what happened to me as a kid.
> He hit us and Mom let him.
>   -Patty, 30, 3rd marriage.

On the other hand, for a few, mixed in with the anger and disappointment of a lost childhood, is a certain amount of understanding flowered by maturity and the experience of living within the same harsh environment which had constrained their parents. As one woman explains her gradual acceptance of her mother;

> I used to blame my mother a lot because
> living at home was so hard and there never
> was any fun or money. It wasn't until I
> got my first divorce and had to raise my
> kid alone that I began to understand how
> things were when I was little.
>   -Sheila, 29, divorced 3 times.

This woman, after years of living, now sees her mother in a different light. She credits her mother with the instillation of certain good qualities in herself, yet still manages to separate herself from her mother.

> Sure, when I look back on myself as a child
> I can now understand how difficult it was
> for my mother. There she was divorced with
> five kids. But her hitting the booze didn't
> help. When I found myself divorced with kids
> to support I was like my mom in some ways.
> Only I got tougher. If she had been tougher
> life would have been better. She taught me
> to be tough because she wasn't.   -Sheila.

For the most part, reflections of the early years concentrated on the disruptions and disharmonies brought about by living in situations dominated by too little money.

> We never had much money to begin with and when Dad lost his job and found out that another baby was on the way, he just split. It was more than he could handle.
> -Lois, 27, divorced 3 times.

> We had to live with my grandparents when I was a kid because my parents were divorced when I was young and she (mother) couldn't make a go of it. My grandparents fought all the time and Mom was gone a lot. I used to wonder what it would have been like if it had been just us.
> -Jean, 27, divorced 3 times.

> There was never any money to go anywhere or do anything-just all of us together in that little house. No wonder people were always fighting-there wasn't anything else to do. No wonder he (the father) left. I left as soon as I could too.
> -Janis, 35, 3rd marriage.

Many blamed lack of money for the exodus of the father or the constant friction caused by a too tired mother.

> There wasn't money enough for booze and to feed us too. He'd rather drink so I guess he left so he didn't have to watch us not have enough. That made it harder even for Mom. At least when he was there, even drunk, he helped out a little.
> Sheila, 29.

The Parental Marriage: Observations of

the Marital Relationship

For many multi-marriers, the parental marriage created a strong impression in young minds. Most of the respondents remembered their parents' marriage, and for many, subsequent remarriages of parents, as relationships which were void of any strong emotional attachment.

What I remember about my parents marriage
is that it wasn't very happy. It seemed
more like a joint partnership to make it
(economically) than a marriage.
               -Frieda, age 35, divorced 3 times.

Very few recall any affection being expressed between
parents and as one man explains:

I never saw them kiss each other or show
that they cared about each other. He
didn't hit her and I suppose they had sex.
They had us children. I don't remember
ever thinking about my father loving my
mother at all. It just wasn't something
that I thought about one way or another.
               -Tom, 39, divorced 2 times.

What did I think of my parents' marriage?
Well, as a child I didn't think of it at
all. But now, in retrospect, I suppose
it was alright. He (the father) ruled with
an iron hand. Mother was sort of in the
background doing what he wanted her to . . .
I guess they were happy enough. At least
my attention was never drawn to the fact
that something was overtly wrong.
               -Charles, 41, 3rd marriage.

The above two responses are from interviews with men.
Women mentally recreate their parents marriage in far
different terms.

I don't call it a marriage--not what I want
a marriage to be. He was an alcoholic and
used to beat us up. I couldn't go to gym
when I was in school because of all the
bruises. He would bring his girlfriends
home with him. My mother would just leave
the room until they left. She divorced
him once when I was three or four. Things
were hard for us then--no money. She
remarried him four years later. When things
were hard when he was gone I used to beg her
to get him back--but when he came back with
all the booze and the beatings, I begged her
to leave him again. She wouldn't. I think
living those years without him scared her.
And living those years with him scared me.
So much of my life was spent in fear of him.

I'm 33 years old and still scared of him.
Their marriage was--he abused and she took
it.
                    -Angela, 3rd marriage.

What marriage do you want to talk about?
I had three step-fathers and never liked
any of them. They were all alcoholics.
All she ever married were alcoholics and
being married to a drinker is no marriage
at all. None of them ever cared if we (the
children) were around.
                    -Lois, 27 divorced 3 times.

     With regard to perceptions of parental marriages,
there is at once a very discernable difference
evidenced between males and females. For females, the
majority of the parental marriages were fraught with
alcohol, physical abuse, extramarital affairs and
little love between parents. Each female was able
to describe in precise terms the quality of relationship she felt her parents employed. For male multi-
marriers, the parental marriage was of little concern.
It existed but few memories are associated with it.
Most males responded to questions concerning the
parental relationship with such phrases as "I guess
they were happy enough, I never thought about it" or
"I suppose he didn't really treat her very well but
she never complained". Even direct probing reveals
little thought on the part of males being given to the
quality of the parental marriage. "You say your
parents had a happy marriage. Could you tell me about
it in a little more depth?"

He never hit her or anything but he did yell
at her on occasion. In retrospect, the only
time I remember him communicating with her
was in direct response to something that
needed to be done. 'I want my dinner now
or pick up my suit at the cleaners'.
Other than that, I don't remember them
talking about anything. But like I said,
she never complained so I guess she was
happy.
                    -Mark, 36, divorced 3 times.

Females, on the other hand, go in to great detail
to illustrate the marriage between parents.

49

Let me tell you what that marriage was like.
When my mother went into the hospital to have
my little brother, my father was out drinking
and went to the hospital drunk. He created
a stink and signed my mother out of the hospital
AMA. He had a friend who worked at a funeral
home so he brought my mother home from the
hospital in a hearse. Can you imagine? I
didn't know if she was dead or what. What
kind of weird father is that? That's the
kind of marriage they had.
                    -Patty, age 30, 3rd marriage.

Notice that for females the descriptions of their
parents' marriage invariably are couched in terms of
the child's relationship with her father. Women began
to illustrate parental marriages with such phrases as
"I hated my father" or "I never got along with my
father". Note the earlier quote cited, "I don't call
it a marriage--at least not what I want a marriage to
be". At that point the woman then began to describe
her relationship with her father as a description of
the parental marriage.

    Male respondents did not speak with this inter-
personal detail. To deny understanding of the parental
marriage (I never thought about it one way or another)
reveals the essence of the male response to the parental marriage. Those marriages existed only peripherially
in the boy's life and had little direct influence on
the day to day activities of the young male multi-
marrier.

    Were the parental marriages of the males so much
better than those of the female? It is doubtful.
Simply because the mother never complained about being
hit or the extra-marital activities of her husband
does not necessarily indicate that the quality of the
marriage was really any better. I believe the answer
lies again in the strong dicotomy between males and
female with regard to interactional perceptions. A
social world is again perceived and experienced differentially. Why do females describe a parental marriage
in relationship to themselves while males show little
intuitive understanding or overt concern with the
parental marriage? Rubin (1976) suggests that being
born male means living in a different world from anything most women know, anything they will ever know.
It means not having to define oneself vicariously
through the lives of others.

Women are socialized into defining the parental marriage in terms of their relationship with a man, in this case, the father or the stepfather. Men are not dependent on relational definitions of the parental marriage and thus show little concern at this time in any intuitive understanding of the parental marriage. It affects them so little. Males and females, while growing up, observed the same qualities in a parental marriage (physical abuse, alcoholism, frequency in exchange of marriage partners) but define these episodes differently. The "bad" parental marriage is of overwhelming concern to the young girl and is well remembered. For the boy, concerned with achievements and sports, the parental marriage is easily ignored.

A Cycle of New Parents

Individuals interviewed for this study were born primarily during the 1940's and grew up during the 1950's. While American society was beginning to experience the effects of a rapidly rising divorce rate during the adolescence of the respondents, an intact family home was still the norm. Divorce had not yet lost its powerfully stigmatizing influence and families who had experienced a divorce were still being termed "broken homes".

During a time period when the intact family home was being heralded as the only appropriate familial form, most multi-marrieds were subjected to the break-up of the home due to divorce. Many divorces were evidenced among the parents of the multi-marrieds. For example, in nine cases where the mother assumed the role of primary singular caretaker, these nine mothers collectively shared 14 divorces. For four other multi-marriers, death of the father and subsequent remarriage by the mother created a restructuring of the family unit during childhood. Two other persons involved in the study were raised by various relatives for sporatic time periods due to incapacity of the mother. In short, not only were multi-marrieds subjected to daily witness of "bad" parental marriages, but for many, this was simply a never-ending cycle of marriage and remarriage, with few episodes of stability on the part of the parents.

Relationships with Parents: Early Interactions

Multi-marriers on the whole generally did not form a close relationship with either parent as a child, and for many, have not yet achieved a sense of intimacy with a parent as an adult. In only one instance did a respondent describe a relationship with a parent as close during childhood. If close-ness does develop over time, it is generally with the mother after the multi-marrier has been out of the family home for many years. This is especially true for males. Fathers are seen as being a member of the traditional "stern father image"; not someone the son can readily relate to. Men, in describing their fathers, are often apt to use words which connote authoritarianism.

> My father was <u>always</u> Sgt. Adams. He was
> a military man. I still think of him
> today as Sgt. Adams.
> 　　　　　-Fred, 37, divorced 4 times.

> My father was a fundamental preacher and
> I guess what I remember most about him was
> his telling me about the things I did
> wrong. I was the black sheep of the family
> and always in trouble and he was always
> talking to me about it.
> 　　　　　-Will, age 30, divorced 5 times.

> My father was real stern. He would beat me
> when I did something wrong. I was always
> a kid to him until the day I married and
> then suddenly I was a man and he never hit
> me again.
> 　　　　　-John, 39, divorced 6 times.

> My father never had time for me as a child.
> He was always working. I played football
> both in high school and college and he
> never once saw me play.
> 　　　　　-Mark, 36, divorced 3 times.

One might ask "Were no fathers open and loving to their sons?" With few exceptions, there appears to be no love and the majority of the relationship of sons with fathers is one which is based on fear. The fathers were conceptualized as authority figures, inflexible and rigid. Fathers were seen as the individuals who meted out punishment and ruled the family with an iron fist. Mothers, on the other hand, were "whispy creatures" living within a mist, not very effective persons and totally devoted to maintenance of hearth and home. However, for most male multi-marriers, it was the mother's home where each sought refuge after divorce.

"After you left your wife, what did you do?"

I went back home to mom's.

"What was your mother's reaction to your divorce?"

You know, that was strange although at the time I didn't think about it that way. It was as if I never left. Life continued on as it always had before and never once did my folks ask me about it or even mention it. It was as if it never happened.
                    -Mark, 35, divorced 3 times.

When my folks found out I was getting a divorce, they came to see me. My father asked me if I was sure this was best. I said yes and he turned to my mother and said. 'See, I told you we couldn't do anything' and then they left and never mentioned it or any of my other divorces again.
                    -Charles, 41, 3rd marriage.

For men, it was as if marriage suddenly elevated them into the ranks of adulthood, a rite of passage, and any subsequent happening in the life of the son was no longer the business of the stern father. The bird had left its nest, and while it could return periodically for rest and recovery, this did not revert the son back into the position of being controlled by the father.

While male multi-marriers generally maintain nominal ties with the mother as adults, the father is quickly discounted as an important person and is seen only inadvertently during visits to the mother. Fear is rapidly forgotten.

For female multi-marriers, the situation is some-what different. The father who is seen as an awesome figure in girlhood still retains that image in adult-

hood. Females, perhaps sensing themselves less powerful, exhibit stronger signs of fear of the forbidding
father.

> I hated my father. I was afraid of him.
>> -Angela, 33.

> I didn't like any of my step-fathers.
> They were all drunks.
>> -Lois, 27.

> When I was 10 my older sister and my mother
> had a talk with me. They told me if my
> father ever tried anything with me to go
> tell them. I was afraid to be in a room
> with him alone.
>> -Patty, 30.

"What was your relationship like with your
mother?"

> My mom was always trying to explain my
> father. She was forever trying to reconcile
> us kids with our father but she never could
> me.
>> -Patty, 30.

> I told you we lived with my grandparents
> until she remarried. She had never learned
> how to cook or keep house because my grand-
> mother always did it. When we moved to the
> new house someone had to do it so I learned
> at the age of nine. My mother never learned
> how. First grandma and then me to do it for
> her.
>> -Jean, 27.

For female multi-marriers, life appeared to be
particularly difficult. As indicated from the
preceding quotes, the majority of female respondents
considered their relationship with their fathers to
be quite bad. The father was seen as an all-powerful
figure and as someone whom they wished to avoid at all
costs. However, unlike their male counterparts who
could more easily justify time spent away from the
home in sports and school activities, being female
denied them the advantage of unaccounted for time
away from the home and insured habitual contact with
the father. Fear of the father was especially
emphasized due to lack of any buffering agents. Most

female multi-marriers denied receiving any support from their mothers during attempts to either avoid interaction or establish any type of working relation- ships with their fathers. A surprising number of females still, after many years, expressed hostility over what they viewed as the lack of buffering by the mother. Reinforced in the still present hostility is the notion that females are ineffectual, powerless compared to men.

> What good was she to me? I told her about
> Dad and the way he was acting towards me
> (sexual overtures) and she wouldn't do any-
> thing. She was always too afraid of him to
> take care of me.
> > -Angela.

> My mother was always too busy with her
> drunks (step-fathers) to worry about us.
> > -Lois.

Several of the female respondents had been reared periodically in the homes of relatives due to chronic psychiatric hospitalizations of their mothers. For these mothers, leniency is evidenced by the child to the extent that an explanation is even supplied as to why the mother is not responsible for memories of an unhappy childhood.

> When my father died I was raised by my aunt.
> My mother was in the hospital. It was so
> hard for her to accept my father's death
> that she needed to be treated for a nervous
> breakdown.
> > -Meg, 39, divorced 5 times.

"Was this her only admission to a hospital?"

Oh, no. Mother was a paranoid schizophrenic. Another woman, again with a mother in the hospital, tells a similar story in defense of her mother.

> After Daddy died mother had problems
> accepting his death and had to be hospitalized
> for nerves. We weren't close because she had
> to go to the hospital. It wasn't her fault
> I wasn't happy. She just couldn't be at home
> because of her nerves.
> > -Martha, 27, divorced 2 times.

It appears that mothers who were not primary caretakers are forgiven for the experiences suffered as a child. Not so mothers who remained in the family home. For the mother who was involved in the child's life on a daily basis, anger is still present for the woman who was not capable of protecting her child from a hostile environment.

Differential Perceptions of Interaction

In terms of relationships with parents, male and female multi-marriers, as adults, recall the parent-child interaction differentially. Fearsome fathers remain scary images for females but lose their potency for males. Mothers are never blamed by sons for beatings or unloving fathers but continue to remain peripheral individuals in the adult's life. Females express such anger towards mothers for the generation of a threatened and insecure childhood, that even as grown women themselves, during this part of the inter-view, tears of bitterness creep out.

Thus, male multi-marriers are taught to respect the strength of the father figure and never give much thought to the role of the mother. Female multi-marriers appeared to develop fairly early a sense of powerlessness over their lives by observing ineffectual mothers as the lesson of superiority on the part of males was replayed over and over. These early concep-tualizations of the roles of men and women in day to day living were destined to be re-enacted during later marriages.

Siblings: The Exclusion of Others in the Meaning

of Family

Few of these individuals were reared in isolation. Most had brothers and sisters sharing the experience of childhood. What of these people? Could they be persons to whom the young multi-marrier could turn for some comfort and security? For the most part, the answer is no. Just as the parental marriage appeared for many multi-marriers to be a "fractured institution" not to be trusted in terms of insuring stability in a relationship, siblings also seemed to be persons the child couldn't trust. Sharing the same growing environment did not justify closeness to the young multi-marrier.

Most individuals interviewed described their relationships with their siblings as not close at all. Many of these persons have little contact with grown siblings now and in giving descriptions of their childhood, seldom volunteered information regarding the existence of any brothers or sisters initially.

"Tell me about your childhood."

Oh, we lived on the farm. My father was a farmer and mother kept house. I liked farm living . . .
                    -Martha, 27, divorced twice.

Approximately 10 minutes later the subject happened to mention a sister.

"You have a sister?"

Oh, yes. I have an older sister and three brothers. Siblings are mentioned only as second thoughts or inadvertently during the discussion of childhood. If a sense of closeness does exist between siblings, it is generally a relationship which has developed since adulthood. For the most part though, little is known about the sibling.

I have two younger brothers.

"How old are they?"

I guess I can give approximate ages. I don't keep track of things like that.
                    -Fred, 37, divorced 4 times.

I manage to see one of my sisters pretty regularly, like at Xmas and things like that. We don't live close to each other so it's hard.
                    -Sheila, 29, divorced 3 times.

"Where does your sister live?"

Across town.

"What is your relationship like with your brothers and sisters?"

My sister is just about it. I figure that's
good enough. One out of five ain't bad.
                                        -Sheila.

    "You say you have a close relationship with one
sister. What about your brothers?"

    Nothing, nothing. They are drinkers, hot
    tempered and physically violent just like
    my father. I stay away from them.

    From the descriptions which are offered of early
childhood, siblings are seen only as a happenstance.
Multi-marriers appear to view siblings much as one
would a survivor in a life boat, haphazardly being
thrown together by fate to share the experience of
being castaways at sea; that is, every man for himself.

    While it is true in most American families that
the parents often remain the primary rallying point
for siblings, at least some ties, however nominal,
are maintained. This is not evident for multi-
marriers. For these individuals the notion of family
is not conceptualized as an enduring relationship
which remains intact much beyond the period of mandatory confinement together. Family, either in the
sense of primary caretaker or membership in the
rearing process, is not portrayed as a stable entity.
Family members come and family members go. Perhaps
the most important lesson multi-marriers learn through
this process of interchangable family members is that
in order to survive within a family context, to be
able to live through it, one had better not place too
much faith in the longevity of relationships.

                   No Place to Call Home

    What becomes apparent in talking with multi-
marriers is the idea that these are people who grew
up essentially alone while living in the midst of
others. As children they were witness to frequent
family fights, often times the observers or the victims
of abuse, and on the whole, suffering from an economic
poverty which is difficult to explain to a child.

    Most of these individuals have few ties with any
one place or any particular set of people. Frequent
moves characterized the geographical arrangements of
the family unit. Primarily this was due to the
necessity on the part of the father or step-father to

secure work. Equally as often mobility was due to
dissolution of the parental marriage.

Nationwide, many children are subjected to
frequent changes of location while living in the
parental home, often with no ill effects. However,
for multi-marriers, already insecure from fractured
emotional involvement with family members, these
moves served only to increase the sense of loneliness.

> My father worked in the oil fields and we
> moved from one oilfield to another. I
> hated that. I never really felt like I
> really belonged. No one really accepted
> me.
> —Lisa, 32, divorced 2 times.

> We were always moving when I was a child.
> Daddy did construction work and we went
> where the jobs were. Everytime I got
> settled in school and began to make friends,
> we moved. I didn't mind moving when there
> was a job to go to, it was the moving in
> the middle of the night because we couldn't
> pay the rent that was the worse.
> —Frieda, 35, divorced 3 times.

> After a while going to school was almost
> funny. In one state I would be six months
> behind and in the next I was one year ahead
> (of my class). It's a wonder I learned to
> read much less finish school.
> —Jeff, 37, 3rd marriage.

Multi-marriers grew up with no ties to any one place.
They lack what Klapp (1975) has referred to as the
symbolic reference points which enable a person to
remember who he is.

> You know, I don't know anyone that I can
> say is a childhood friend. We moved so
> much I never got to really know anyone
> and no one knew me.
> —Meg, 39, divorced 5 times.

Multi-marriers, on the whole, seldom lived in one
locality very long. Subject to frequent moves, often
for embarrassing reasons such as nonpayment of rent,
these persons have no memories which tie them to one
particular place. They have no sense of roots, no

sense of belonging.

The Effects of Disrupted Interactions:

A Loss in Identity

Klapp (1975) states that

excessive mobility also makes family relations
fragile which, of course, strikes at the
heart of identity. Divorce, serial marriage,
desertion of children, alienation of youth
from parents, dispersion of kin, insecurity
of old people deprive a person of the ability
to define himself by relations which should
be most reliable, intimate, and meaningful
(p. 45).

Multi-marriers are deprived of the intimate relationships, of the treasured recollections of childhood
hiding places and swings, which help aid a person to
gain stability in dealing with the world and give to
that person a sense of identity, a way of knowing who
they are.

This lack of a sense of identity due to interchangable homes staffed by interchangable people is
evidenced readily when one glances at the relationships between divorced parents who leave and children
still living within the home. Landis (1950) pointed
to the high divorce rate beginning in the United
States and commented on the distinction between
serial polygamy and serial monogamy. In terms of
maintaining some type of ties with the former spouse,
most Americans practice some form of serial polygamy.
Child support, however sporatic, is generally paid.
Occasional discussions between parents occur regarding
the future of the children take place and most
divorced parents still take at least nominal interest
in the children who are left behind.

Serial monogamy, in the strictest sense, is
evidenced among the homes which spawned multi-marriers.
With few exceptions, once the tie is broken legally,
in terms of divorce, parents, usually fathers, leave
and are never seen or heard from again.

My father left when I was eight and I have
never seen him again.
-Lois, 27, divorced twice.

"Have you looked for him?"

Not as an adult. As a child I used to go
to bars where he hung out to see if he might
still go there, but then we moved, and I
stopped thinking about him.

My parents were divorced when I was born.
I never knew my father. A few years ago
I happened to be back in the town my mother
grew up in and someone pointed out my father
to me.
                    -Jean, 27, divorced twice.

"Did you go up to him and meet him?"

No, he didn't have anything to do with me
when I was young, so why now?

If the early homelife was particularly painful, often
it is the children who initiate their own form of
serial monogamy with parents.

My mother was no great mother when I was
growing up. Last mother's day I did call
her and take her out to lunch but that was
the first time I had seen her in ten years.
                    -Sheila, 29, divorced three times.

Multi-marriers grow up with no sense of belonging,
either to a place or a set of people. Relationships
are quickly set aside and seldom taken up again.
Parents, brothers, sisters and childhood acquaintances
are left behind as one era in a person's life ends
and another begins. In short, long term interpersonal skills, those necessary for securing enduring
relationships, are not observed by the child and
appear not to be internalized in the repertoire of
life experiences.

Summary: The Negated Search for Self

Through Family

Weigert and Hastings (1977) describe the function
of the family in terms of its importance to the
development of an integrated sense of self.

The basic relationships of the nuclear
family, viz., conjugal love, parental support

61

or filial piety, and sibling ties, are
central to the processes of identity
formation. The relevant characteristics
of these relationships are that they are
particularistic, normatively defined by
self and others as involving positive affect,
generally requiring intense and frequent
fact-to-face interaction, and based on
cumulative and implicit background expectancies;
thus they constitute a socially and personally
defined reality with a unique history, a
recognizable collective identity, and mutual
claims project into the future. In a word,
the family is a 'world', albeit a little one,
in which selves emerge, act, and acquire a
stable sense of identity and reality (p. 1172).

In terms of the purpose and importance of the family
as described by Weigart and Hastings, multi-marriers,
as children, were not privy to the elements necessary
for the nuturing of a stable sense of identity and
reality, at least to the extent this sense of self
applies to the process of long-term familial
relationships.

Both men and women learn during the early years
that relationships are transitory at best and at
worst are quickly cast aside as the situation alters.
These are people who have grown up within the midst
of poverty, cruelty and instability. A strong sense
of identity with people or places is lacking and for
the large part, isolation is the end result. Multi-
marriers grow up lonely and for males, we see a
turning outward, away from the social world of
relationships. Females, cast aside in a sea of
ever-changing fathers, learn to view themselves in
terms of the social world of relationships, however,
never quite finding any one person who is permanent
enough with which to form a close tie.

Childhood, for these people, is preferred forgotten, for memories are painful and still generate
hurt. In coming chapters, we shall see how childhood messages influence interaction as adults. We
will see how the instability of relationships in
early life create a standard by which multi-marriers
compare, to a certain degree, their present lives.

The early years for multiple marriers were,
indeed, hard years. Confusion, isolation, physical

and emotional pain, alienation from family, loss of a
sense of identity due to frequent relocations and
frequent changing of family members characterized for
most part the memories of childhood. Children learned
not to place faith in such things as relationships,
not to commit themselves to an entity which is fragile
and lacking in substance. Perhaps Farber's (1964)
concept of permanent availability is reinforced at
this time.

For males, throughout the course of childhood, we
see young men who grow up and place more value on
individual goals, goals which have little to do with
the inclusion of relationships as a mechanism for
measuring success. Females, whose childhood was
characterized by an increasing sense of powerlessness,
come to view themselves primarily in terms of their
relationships with men. A decline in the importance
of others, as fundamental in the meaning of family,
is emphasized.

CHAPTER IV

FIRST MARRIAGES: BEGINNINGS AND ENDINGS

Udry (1966, p. 1) writes that "of all the different
kinds of human relationship, each society tends to
emphasize one which has particular significance to its
organization".   Given the social forces of industriali-
zation and urbanization which have been dominant since
the emergence of the United States, the primary ideal
family type to be institutionalized within this Western
culture is that of the conjugal family unit (Goode,
1963).   While the changing economic situation within
the United States has begun to loosen the stereotypical
framework within which this conjugal family operates,
it is still marriage, as representative of a conjugal
family form, which is institutionalized and accepted as
the right and proper relationship for individuals to
assume as a lifestyle commitment.

The conjugal relationship is so institutionalized
within this society that it still remains as one of
the few acts participated in which legitimately notes
a rite of passage.   We identify marriage as the normal
status for adults to assume and we socialize our young
to achieve this status at some time in their lives.
Over 95 percent of all Americans marry at some time and
for many females, marriage is "the singularly acceptable way to move from girl to woman"   Rubin, 1976, p.
41).   Marriage, with its ability to bestow adult status
on participants, occupies a privileged status among the
significantly validating relationships for adults in
our society.

Marriage, as a cultural tradition and directive,
influences us to come to the understanding that the
marital relationship is the one truly legitimate way
to participate in on-going society as full members and
as adults.   Berger and Kellner have referred to marriage as the crucial nomos building instrumentality
in our society.   They state that it is on the basis of
marriage that, for most adults in our society, existence
in the private sphere is built up (Berger and Kellner,
1974).   From a higher level of analysis, marriage is
representative of the established ways of organizing
and participating in family life.

A more individualistic analysis of marriage shows
that, for most adults, marriage is necessary in the
creation and maintenance of a particular social
identity which is employed for participating in on-going

society. "Marriage is the social arrangement that creates for the individual that sort of order in which he can experience his life as making sense" (Berger and Kellner, 1974, p. 219). Marriage is necessary for the organization and playing out of interaction in a validly recognized fashion. In short, "the spouses mutually bestow particular and intensely affective identities as unique biographical realities" (Weigert and Hasting, 1977, p. 1172).

Marriage, while co-existing in mutually inclusive categories, can be examined from two perspectives. Marriage, as a cultural directive, influences us to come to the understanding that the marital relationship is the right and proper status to assume as participating adults in greater society. Marriage can also be seen as a necessary prerequisite in the presentation of social identities in a social world of interaction. Throughout the course of this chapter, this dual faceted nature of marriage plays an important part in the decision making' processes of multi-marriers. Differentially, according to sex, entering into the marital relationship is seen as responding to a particular role obligation arising from a cultural directive and as a mandatory component of a social self. From either point of analysis, a micro or a macro perspective, marriage produces "a world without which the individual is powerfully threatened with anomie in the fullest sense of the word" (Berger and Kellner, 1974, p. 231).

Despite the quality of family life observed by the young multi-marriers growing up in an environment of alcohol, physical violence, family hostilities, and disrupted family units, multi-marriers were very responsive to the compelling call for marriage. These individuals entered into first marriages at a relatively young age. Female multi-marriers first married between the ages of 16 and 20, with 18 being the average age at first marriage. Males, marrying for the initial time between the ages of 17 and 22, entered their first marriage around the average age of 19.

Given the circumstances of these individuals experiences with family life, why were they so intent on marriage that they first approached it at relatively tender years? In talking with these persons, the answer becomes quite clear. Multi-marriers marry for the first time for all the same reasons that everyone else in the United States marries. They respond to role obligations and seek to immerse themselves with others for the purpose of creating a sense of self. However, in following the progression of these young people into first marriages, it becomes evident that these people, as a category of persons, are so completely responsive to cultural demands that viable options to marriage are simply not perceived. For them, to actively engage in on-going society with full rights and privileges, marriage is mandatory. The concept of choice is not a crucial element in the meaning of marriage. That they will marry is a given, it is only the matter of who they will marry which is at times problematic.

First marriages, as explored in this chapter, are examined in order to come to some understanding of the interplay of culture and social meanings as they are experienced by multi-marriers.

As noted earlier, there is a difference between males and females in the decision making processes involved in entering the first marriage. This difference is a result of the strong differential process of socialization into sex roles experienced in childhood. These various orientations to "doing" and "being" (Chodorow, 1971) give rise to varying meanings applied to marriage by males and females. Ultimately the final decisions to enter into and depart from the first marriage are enacted differently according to the perception of social worlds as seen and experienced by males and females. Thus, understanding of first marriages as expressed and experienced by multi-marriers is presented as a function of gender identification.

The First Marriage for Males:

An Acquiescence to Roles

Male multi-marriers tend to explain their motivations for entering the first marriage almost by appeal to higher authority, that of cultural directive. Most regard this marriage to be the result of outside forces operating on them, forcing them into a decision to marry, as if they themselves had been rendered ineffectual in the face of opposition.

I went into service right after high school. I met my first wife when I came back from service. She was 16 and working part-time as a car hop. I went to the restaurant where

she was working and met her there. I was
20 at the time. We dated and then got
married.
                    -Fred, age 37, divorced 4 times.

"How long did you date?"

About a month.

"Did you want to get married? Is that why you
dated for such a short time?

No, not really. You see, I was brought up
to believe that if you have sex you get
married.

"So you married because you were having sex with
her?"

No, not completely. I was made aware of
a pregnancy and that on top of having sex
made me get married.

Several of the male participants in this study described pre-marital pregnancies as the motivation for
first marriages. Each marriage was conceptualized as
a particular situation which forced them into a
marriage which would not have occurred otherwise. "I
had to get married" or "I got caught" were the words
most frequently used to illustrate the perceived lack
of choice on the part of the male. Religion is also
utilized as a coercive factor in the decision to
marry.

I was 17 and she was 15 when we ran off and
got married. We had to get married.
                    -John, age 39, divorced 6 times.

"Had to? You mean she was pregnant?"

No, she wasn't pregnant. But we had had
sex. I was taught if you had sex then you
had to get married. She was the first girl
I had ever touched so I had to marry her.

Often men describe their marriages as the result of
being pushed into it by social pressure.

She was a beauty queen in high school, very
social person. We dated on and off for four

67

years of high school. It was a very stormy
relationship--fighting a lot and making up
again. Not dating each other for a while
and then getting back together. We married
while I was in college.
                -Mark, age 36, divorced 3 times.

"Why did you decide to marry?"

I think it was just expected of us. We had
gone together for so long that it was the
right thing to do. I didn't have any desire
to get married, but everybody was waiting
for us to get married, since we had survived
high school and all, that it seemed like the
thing to do.

Another man attributes his marriage to much the
same reasons.

I married her while we were in college. She
was very bright but just didn't want to go to
college. We had dated for those years in
high school--so when I went to college it
was just assumed I'd take her with me.
Looking back, I don't know why I got married.
I suppose it was because it was expected of
us.
-Charles, 41, presently in third marriage.

For males, the first marriage is defined as a
capitulation to social pressure. No one married
because they, as individuals, wanted to marry. All
present themselves as victims of social coersion.
Each was fulfilling the expectations of peer groups
or families. Occasionally someone would plead compli-
ance to a higher authority, God, and state that sexual
intercourse was a mandate for marriage, but no one
extended the traditional rationale, love, as a
motivation for first marriages. Even with prodding,
love was only superficially employed as motivating
factor in marriage.

"You said you had to get married because it was
expected. Did you love her?"

Oh, I don't know about love. There was this
sexual attraction . . .
                -Jeff, age 37, in third marriage.

I guess I might have thought I was in love
but then you are supposed to think you are.
            -Will, age 30, divorced 5 times.

I cared about her. You are supposed to care
about the people you marry.
            -Fred, age 37, divorced three times.

No one married for love. If love, in some vague form,
did exist, it was characterized as neither necessary
or sufficient condition for marriage. Marriage was
entered into as the proper response to a given set of
societal conditions, a way of fulfilling expectations
concerning a particular situation. Men were doing
their duty in essence, at least in terms of societal
expectations. Men simply did not identify this
marriage as being in any way related to personal or
emotional needs. Marriage was conceptualized as a
set of role obligations one entered into in a contrac-
tual sense. There is no indication that marriage, as
a personal experience in making sense of one's world,
was entered into with the understanding that the spouse
would play any significant part in the sustaining of
a social identity. Marriage was viewed as a separate
structure from any component part of one's real life.
One simply married when one was expected to marry and
not because the marriage partner was seen as being
responsible for personal happiness.

Marriage as Distinct from Self

This idea of the separateness of marriage from
personal experience is seen again. When asking male
multi-marriers about their expectations of marriage,
one is again left with a constricted definition of
marriage in the male scheme of things.

I had no idea what to expect out of marriage.
I had never thought about it. I guess I
expected it to be like . . . marriage. You
know, marriage.
                    -Fred, age 37.

"What do you mean by 'marriage'?"

I don't know. I just never thought about it.

Another describes his same lack of understanding
regarding the concept of marriage as a relationship.

> I never thought about what it would be like
> to be married. I only thought about how I
> had to get married.
> > -Tom, 39, divorced twice.

One man did have certain expectations regarding his
marriage although still no real emphasis was placed on
marriage as a relationship between he and his spouse.

> I had no real idea about what marriage
> would be like when I married her. I
> guess I expected things to settle down
> somewhat. I thought because we were
> married things wouldn't be so stormy.
> > -Mark, age 37, divorced 3 times.

"Why did you think things wouldn't be so stormy
after you married?"

> Because things are supposed to settle down
> once you're married.

Marriage to male multi-marriers is an interesting
phenomenon. It is viewed as an act which one partici-
pates in and subsequently places on a shelf. All gave
credence to the notion that one is indeed expected to
fulfill his obligations by discharging this act at
the appropriate time, but no one had given any thought
to how one goes about the process of engaging in
marriage on a day to day basis. The concept of
marriage as anything more than a state of affairs,
much like the weather or one's political party, was
not given much introspection. Marriage is something
that exists "out there", having very little to do with
social interaction.

Udry (1966) has addressed the notion that
Americans do not know what happens after marriage. As
he explains it:

> The ignorance of marital processes for the un-
> married is soci logically quite understandable:
> As a child, one interacts with parents within
> a parent-child relationship. There is little
> in this interaction which gives a child much
> insight into the husband-wife relationship
> from which he is excluded. Furthermore, he
> can only observe his parents from the vantage
> point of his role as child and their role as
> parents to him (p. 269).

Udry further goes on to point out that ignorance of
what constitutes the process of marriage aids in the
creation of two opposing myths regarding marriage
which are believed in simultaneously: the myth of
living happy ever after and the myth of the drudgery
of marriage.

This notion of ignorance regarding the marital
relationship is seen very clearly when one examines
the various related expectations of marriage. Men, on
the whole, simply did not know what to expect of
marriage. Given the fact that most men felt coerced
into marriage and did not conceptualize marriage as
being personally related to individual happiness, it
is probably a safe assumption to suggest that these
male multi-marriers were more cognizant of marriage
as drudgery than as a state of perpetual happiness
ever after.

This notion on the part of men that marriage
exists but is of little personal consequence was
seen earlier in this study in the chapter on the early
years of multi-marriers. Female multi-marriers were
acutely aware of their parent's marriages, to the
point that they described the parental marriage in
relational terms with themselves. Men on the other
hand, acknowledged the existence of the parents
marriage, but felt that it had very little to do with
them personally. Marriage, like family members in the
early home, is again only a peripheral component in
one's life.

For male multi-marriers, the first marriage
then, is seen as a static state of affairs. It is
an act which is to be accomplished, not continually
played out on a daily basis. You do marriage by
getting married. Men don't see themselves as being
married in the sense that one constructs the marriage
out of joint action.

Given the fact that the first marriage is viewed
as little more than fulfillment of role obligations,
it should not be surprising to see this view of
marriage as drudgery reenacted within the marriage
relationship itself.

I'll tell you what that marriage was like.
Pure hell. I was in college and she resented
the fact that she had to work while I was
in school. She wanted more money. She

71

never understood that I was trying to make
things work out. I was planning for a
future. I was going to school during the
day, working at night and going to foot-
ball practice all at the same time. She
wanted more things, like she wanted to go
out a lot, to the movies and parties. I
didn't have time for that. I was planning
for a future, for both of us but she never
understood that.
                    -Mark, 37, divorced 3 times.

My marriage was really bad. For the ten
years I was married it was always the same.
I worked all the time and then when I did
get off work I went to shoot pool and drink
beer with the guys. I didn't want to go
home and play with the kids, cut the grass
and make a garden. I hate all those things.
My marriage was that I was just providing
and bringing home the bacon. The truth is,
I didn't want to be there, I just didn't
want to be home at all. It wasn't fun at
home. It was fun at the pool hall.
                    -Fred, 37, divorced 5 times.

Our marriage was pretty strange. She
wanted me to get a daytime job and act
like a real husband. We had different
goals in life. It was like the fun seemed
to stop. After we got married all of a
sudden it was legal and she wanted everything to be real legal-like traditional.
I hated it.
                    -David, 30, divorced 2 times.

In listening to men describe their first marriages,
one is left with a sense of sorrow mixed slightly with
humor. The situation is reminiscent of Freud's
confusion when he stated with frustration, "What does
a woman want?" The implication by these men is clear.
"I married her so what more does she want?"

     Male multi-marriers, at least in terms of the
ways they approached their first marriages, did not
appear to have any understanding that the marital
relationship would need to be negotiated. The taking
of the vow constituted the totality of the concept
marriage, and it appears that these men somehow
expected their wives to adjust to their lifestyle.

It simply never occurred to them that their spouses might have expectations regarding marriage which they had not considered.

McAllister (1963) suggests that differential expectations regarding marriage partners may be created with the emergence of marital roles.

> We all have preconceived ideas of what a
> husband should be like, and what a wife
> should be like; we forget that someone
> else is playing the role, someone else
> has the stage, someone else is ad libbing
> his way through a difficult scene. The
> real problem, of course, is that in the
> individual marriage, each spouse has a
> mental picture of how the other spouse
> should fulfill his role (p. 153).

Thus, we see male multi-marriers entering into a relationship which is based on a conceptualization of marriage as drudgery with firmly entrenched role expectations regarding their wives' participation.

This notion of rigid role expectations is seen in the short dating period most men engaged in prior to marriage. Many men dated their first wives for only a few months prior to marriage and those that had engaged in lengthy courtship described these relationships as on and off with long periods of not dating between episodes of dating. When asked if any discussion regarding marriage occurred between them and their prospective wives prior to marriage, the answer was always no. These men entered a relationship with no clearly defined strategy for interaction and with very little sense of "self" inserted in the definition. Marriage is seen as something that just happens. Marriage, for them, is a state, not a process.

The First Divorce: Relinquishing

Role Obligations

Considering the enormous amout of complacency evidenced by these men in adhering to role sets by marrying, it would not be surprising to find that leaving the marriage, i.e., abdicating responsibility, would be a painful experience. For the most part, this is true for the first marriage. Very few left the first marriage without a great deal of personal struggle and agony.

I knew I wasn't happy at home. I hated
being there but leaving was hard too. I
remember getting up in the middle of the
night, putting on the Willie Nelson albums,
drinking to dawn, going to work and coming
home and doing the same thing all over again.
I felt so guilty about wanting to leave her.
When I finally did leave, it was a drawn
out thing-moving out and moving in over and
over.

            -Fred, age 37, divorced 3 times.

"If you didn't want to be there, why was it so
hard to leave?"

I felt responsible for her. She didn't have
an education or any experience. How was she
going to take care of herself? It wasn't
right to leave someone alone--she was like
a baby.

Or

Our marriage had deteriorated to the point
that I felt there had to be something better
than this. I couldn't go on in those
circumstances. I owed myself more. There
had to be more to life than this. So I
left, finally, after we had separated many
times . . . We separated so many times
because I just couldn't leave her cold like
that. I needed to get her prepared. I had
married her and it wasn't right to just walk
out on her unannounced. She needed time to
look out for herself.
            -Charles, age 41, third marriage.

The dissolution of the first marriage was
characterized by frequent separations prior to the
final act of divorce. Despite high levels of dissatisfaction and unhappiness with the marriage and the
spouse, it was simply not possible for these men to
walk out on their role obligations without a great deal
of thought. It was necessary to prepare their wives
for their eventual departures. The problem was not
in the decision to leave, that decision was firm. The
delicacy of the situation revolved around the timing
and the gracefulness of the exit. Each man felt the
heavy weight of obligation to marriage and wished to
leave in such a way as to minimize that load, by somehow insuring that the wife he no longer wanted could

survive without him. Considering the fact that most
had entered the marriage due to a strong adherance to
societal norms, males felt that one should discard
that dedication with the least amount of destruction
possible.

In examining the decision-making process on the
part of males to divorce, the attitude that marriage
is not conceptualized as an interpersonal relationship to be negotiated is manifested again.

"When you realized that you were unhappy, did you
discuss this with your wife or anyone else?"

> No, I never talked to her about it. I
> was the one unhappy. There wasn't any
> reason to talk to her about it.
> > -Mark, age 36.

> I don't believe in marriage counseling.
> Either a marriage works or it doesn't.
> Talking about it isn't going to change
> anything.
> > -Jeff, age 37.

> There wasn't any point in talking to her
> or anyone else about it. The only way
> things could change to make me happy was
> by my changing--learning to like living
> the way we were--and I wasn't going to,
> had no plans to change. So there wasn't
> any point in talking about it.
> > -Will, age 30.

> A man just doesn't talk about things like
> that. You just make your decision and
> stick to it. I was unhappy and wanted out
> and needed to make sure she was taken care
> of. When that was done then I could just
> leave. Talking about things don't change
> them.
> > -Fred, age 37.

The decision to leave is played out in the shadow
of a "John Wayne caricature". A man's gotta do what
a man's gotta do. You do it as gently as possible but
you certainly don't talk about it. The orientation is
towards action and talk is not conceived of as action.
Leaving is action and man's work. Talking is woman's
work.

This notion that wives are somehow supposed to adjust themselves to the husband's life with a minimal amount of complication is seen also by this inability of men to talk with their wives about their marriages.

"You never told your wife you were unhappy?"

No. There wasn't any point to it. She was happy. I wasn't. She liked being married. I didn't. I guess she knew I was unhappy. I was hell to live with, but there wasn't anything to discuss. She liked it. I didn't. What more can you say about it?
                                    -Fred, age 37.

Indeed, what more can be said about it. It never seemed to occur to these men that perhaps the marriage relationship could be changed, somehow negotiated. Marriage was seen as one of the true "givens" in life, unalterable and impregnable. One buys a suit and then either wears it if it fits well or discards it if it doesn't. To have a suit tailored to fit well is inconceiveable.

Thus, for male multi-marriers, marriage is an institutional burden one assumes when one accepts adult status in society. These men so little understood the notion that marriage should be an expression also of personal satisfaction that they never discussed with their wives their views on what constitutes a marriage. It was simply assumed that wives must indeed hold the same frame of reference as they.

First Marriage for Females

Marriage as Self

Female multi-marriers were also tuned into the structural component of marriage within society. They understood that marriage was a reflection of adult status and responsibility. However, they, unlike their male counterparts, emphasized the interpersonal nature of the marital relationship as being equal if not more important than the awesome fulfillment of role obligations. Remember, even as young girls these women showed a tendency to express their social worlds in relational terms.

Most females carried with them into the marriage certain expectations of the rewards that marriage

76

would bring. They, unlike their male counterparts,
appear to believe in the myth of marriage meaning
happiness ever after.

> I expected from marriage a home, family,
> my own little place. I think I expected
> the good part of my home as a child without
> the bad parts.
> -Sheila, 29, divorced 3 times.

> For as long as I can remember I had always
> wanted a washer, a dryer, and six kids.
> -Martha, 26, divorced 2 times.

> I wanted security and a happy little
> relationship.
> -Lois, 27, divorced 3 times.

Even for those females who stated they entered their
first marriages as an escape mechanism from a bad
home situation, still implied in their comments are
touches of relational concepts.

> I had been going to college and I didn't
> really know what to do in life so I got
> married. I wanted to change him. I wanted
> to show him what family life was like. I
> figured if he was happy in a family then
> he would settle down.
> -Martha, age 26.

> When I married I probably didn't know what
> I really did want because I had never been
> around a good marriage long enough to see
> what they were about. I just thought that
> if I got married I would have some security.
> I had never had any security and marriage
> meant security. Just one person to love
> me and care about me.
> -Lois, 27, divorced 3 times.

> I never really thought about what I expected
> out of marriage. I had planned to just move
> in with him after high school. But my family
> thought sin, sin, sin and insisted we get
> married. I just wanted to be with him all
> the time so we got married.
> -Jean, 27, divorced 2 times.

I loved him and I loved the way he made me

77

feel. Until that time I didn't think my
existence had ever contributed to anyone's
happiness. I wanted to marry him. I
didn't know, didn't think what to expect
out of marriage. I just wanted to be with
him.
                    -Frieda, 35, divorced 3 times.

        Marriage for female multi-marriers was seen as
an act which would bring to them a certain amount of
personal happiness whether it resulted from the
security marriage appeared to offer to them or as
the end product of being with someone they cared
about. Marriage was undertaken primarily to insure
relationships, not primarily to answer role
obligations.

        From a very young age females are taught to
expect men to care for them, take care of them and
insure personal happiness. Even if a woman is unhappy
in the parental home, the tying oneself legally to a
man is often seen as the only effective way to leave
the home.

        Because of the way I was raised, in a
        physically violent home, I had to leave
        home. I had to get away from there. I
        couldn't leave home until I was married.
        You just weren't supposed to leave home
        until you married so I married.
                    -Angela, 33, married 3 times.

        I got married at 16. I had run away from
        home several times. I was scared of the
        beating at home and all that crap. I
        knew running away wasn't going to work.
        Everytime I ran away they brought me home.
        They kept putting me back in the house so
        suddenly I realized if I was married I
        could leave. So I tricked him (the first
        husband). I got pregnant, got married,
        and left home.
                    -Patty, 30, married 3 times.

        For men, marriage was seen primarily as an
institution which had little direct meaning in terms
of considering the other partner as important in one's
life. Females were expected to adjust their lives to
their husbands. Female multi-marriers very closely
identified with the importance of the "other" in the

marriage relationship. They firmly understood that
the marriage did not exist without the necessary
"other". Marriage was undertaken not to fulfill the
expectations of society but to fulfill expectations of
themselves. Being married, not simply getting married,
represented to them their ascendency into the adult
role. To be away from home, to be with someone, to
be in a happy home all emphasized the processes
involved in the marital relationship. That "other",
a man, was necessary for the fulfilling of personal
goals. The presence or absence of the man as the
means whereby they judged personal happiness is
evidenced at a young age.

> Diary entry, at age 18
> November 12, 1963
> I just haven't felt like writing in here
> lately. When the blues come they come full
> force and they did today. I'm so mixed up
> that I don't think I will ever get myself
> organized. All I want is . . . what? I
> think sometimes I'll keep traveling around
> and live, live, live. Then I wonder if I
> shouldn't go to college and make something
> of myself. There's the family part too,
> do I want a husband, family, and my own
> home? Confusion is enough to drive you
> to frustration and tears.
>   -Frieda.

Exhibited in this diary entry is the confusion of a
young girl as she seeks an adequate place in society
for herself. Does she want a man or does she want
to live, live, live? Her next diary entry suggests
that perhaps her personal happiness is dependent on a
man and marriage.

> November 15, 1963
> Well, I can honestly say that I am happy
> now. I hope it lasts forever. I have been
> happy and have had a peace of mind--Night
> before last I got a cable from Dale . . .
> I would be so happy to have an adoring
> husband and later-children.

Still later

> May 18, 1964
> I hope I someday find someone to love and
> who will love me just as much. The harder
> I look the dimmer the future looks. From

here on, time plays the cards and God willing
I'll love and marry.

December 24, 1964
I get so lonely sometimes that I would give
the world for someone to call my own. I
want a family and a baby boy and a home.

Marriage as an Adjustment

Noted earlier was the assumption on the part of
the male multi-marrier that his wife would somehow
adjust her life to his without the need for very much
discussion on the matter. To a large extent, female
multi-marriers do indeed attempt to master this
adjustment.

Several noted family sociologists have commented
on this tendency on the part of women to adjust to
their husbands. As Bernard (1972) explains this
phenonomen:

Because the wife has put so many eggs into
the one basket, of marriage, to the exclusion
of almost every other, she has more at stake
in making a go of it. If anything happens
to that one basket, she loses everything;
she has no fallback position. She tends,
therefore, to have to make more of the
concessions called for by it (p. 44).

Burgess and Wallin (1953) found that the husband, upon
marriage, maintains his old life routines, with no
thought or expectation of changing them to suit his
wife's wishes. Sometimes, when the wife concedes
that the husband has made more adjustments, he reports
himself to be quite unaware of making any; they were
probably too trivial for him to notice.

Women understand the extent to which they will
be expected to adjust to their husband's lifestyle.
Most women are successful to some degree in this
attempt to mold oneself to the husband's desires.
Female multi-marriers, on the whole, appeared willing
to go to great lengths in order to make the transition
into their husband's world; their need to be tied to
a man is so strong.

So dependent is their identity on the marital
relationship that rather potent redefinitions of

situations occur spontaneously during this adjustment phase. Note again a diary entry from the same young woman. At this time she has met her first husband and plans to shortly marry.

> January 16, 1966
> I know he loves me and wants me. We don't always kiss like we used to or pledge our love 30 times a night but I have never been happier than now because I've learned how he gives love and I've learned how he accepts my love. He'll call me Ace and I know I'm his best friend and he'll hold me and I'll cry because I know he loves me with all he has to love with. I still give my love like I used to but I've found how to interpret his words and actions correctly and now I know a slap on the rear means he loves me . . . He gives love in a way completely foreign to me but that's ok now--because I've learned to accept him and his actions and not be impatient when he doesn't express himself as I do. He bitches and complains about my driving--so he's letting me know I mean enough to him to worry about. He gets impatient when I eat too much--fine he loves me enough to want to show me off (but I gotta be slender). He sits and watches TV and never says boo to me--I know he can feel satisfied and happy just being in the same room with me. He falls asleep but I don't get mad--not anymore. I think who else can he feel so relaxed around and trust as much as me--no one. That's a grand kind of compliment . . .

Decisions to Marry

Like male multi-marriers, females were also prone to marry after very short courtships. Many marriages occurred on the spur of the moment.

> I was living in a garage apartment with my girlfriend. Doug lived down below us. I knew him for several weeks. One night there was a party I went to with Doug. We got pretty drunk and Doug said 'Why don't we get married?' so our friends convinced us to wait until the next morning when we were sober. I slept with him that night and the next morning we decided to go ahead

and get married. I wanted my own home and
husband. So we got married.
                    -Janis, age 35, in third marriage.

There I was. I couldn't afford college,
I didn't have a job, I hated living at home.
Doug and I had dated during high school on
and off. He was ready to get married. I
wanted security, security, security so I
figured if I got married I would finally
have a home of my own and someone of my
own.
                    -Lois, 27, divorced 3 times.

I had dated my first husband for two years
before. I didn't really like him all that
much but he wanted to get married. I had
finished college then and was teaching high
school. I didn't really like teaching. I
wanted my own children and a home of my own.
So when I broke up with this other man I
had been dating, someone I really cared about,
I was hurt and looking for someone to love
me. Back into my life stepped Carl, swearing
he would always love me. So I thought I
wasn't getting any younger so we got married.
                    -Lisa, 32, divorced twice.

Most female multi-marriers entered into the first
marriage without deep consideration, often spontaneously. Marriages were frequently utilized as a mechanism
for exiting from a bad situation which was generating
unhappiness. Rubin (1976) states that for many young
working class girls, getting married was, and probably
still is, the singularly acceptable way out of an
oppressive family situation and into a respected social
status. No matter how escape ridden the motivation
for marriage, each entered into the marriage with
deeply held expectations. Each had some notion that
marriage, the joining of herself with a man, would
result in increased personal happiness. Most females
simply expected that an emotional bonding between
themselves and their husbands would occur no matter
what the circumstances surrounding the initiation into
marriage. These women, just like their male counterparts, worked on the assumption that the prospective
spouses held the same convictions regarding marriage
as they did, the difference being that females operated on a lower level of analysis, with an expectation
that the marital relationship would enhance them

personally by completing a social identity. They
appeared to understand that marriage involved some
type of joint action but even so, it was assumed
that their husbands also operated with the same understanding. Females, like males, did not discuss marriage roles and expectations prior to marriage with
their spouses either.

Being Married: The Failure of

Marriage Expectations

As previously mentioned, male multi-marriers
entered the first marriage expecting wives to naturally adjust to their lifestyles. Females entered marriage intuitively ready for accommodation, understanding that a certain amount of adjustment on their
part would be called for. The concept of marriage as
a joint act was already in effect. Most assumed that
given their willingness to accommodate their husbands,
the marriage should fulfill expectations and bring a
certain level of contentedness. However innocent,
none suspected prior to marriage that such an arrangement would not work out.

> Our marriage was very one-sided as far as
> interests went. He was active in Demolay
> and other organizations. He was into
> politics so I went to political meetings
> with him and sat in motel rooms reading
> when he didn't need me for cocktail parties.
> We went to his parents home every free week-
> end. I didn't really enjoy all that but I
> thought that that was what a good wife
> was supposed to do. I thought if I did
> everything real well and supported him he
> would come to need me in his life.
> -Lisa, 32, divorced twice.

> He was a real nice guy, a good person and
> he always wanted to do the right thing.
> When I found out I was pregnant he married
> me. I just wasn't happy in the marriage.
> I wanted a real job and all. He kept
> telling me it was my duty to stay at home
> and raise the kid so I kept trying to be
> happy doing that. I felt there was some-
> thing wrong with me because I wasn't happy
> doing that.
> -Sheila, 29, divorced three times.

Each woman was determined initially to make the marriage work. So dedicated to the notion that a happy marriage was dependent on adjustment to their husband's wishes, that several went to extremes in order to fulfill this expectation.

> Several months after we were married he
> started hitting me. I was pretty mouthy
> and wouldn't do everything he wanted me to.
> When I talked back to him, he would hit me.
> I guess I deserved being beaten. I tried
> to learn not to talk back to him.
> —Janis, third marriage.

> My husband expected me to wait on him hand
> and foot. I had a full time job too but
> it was still me that did the housework
> and cooking and everything else. One day
> I was out working in the garden and he was
> watching a game on TV and he called me in
> to get him another beer from the refrigerator.
> I did it. I thought that was what a good
> wife was supposed to do for her husband.
> —Angela, third marriage.

Despite the high level of domestic and subservient behavior expected of them by their husbands, female multi-marriers related that they would have stayed in those marriages. Even being beaten was seen as a way of being taught the correct adjustment to their husbands. They perceived their unhappiness with the marriage to somehow be their fault, due to their inability to perform adequately as wives, or make the appropriate adjustments.

The Decision to Divorce

Female multi-marriers, like their male counterparts, generally were the initiators of divorce. Considering the extreme measures they were willing to undertake to insure a successful marriage, it is insightful to note the reasons they give for the decision to end their marriages.

> Our marriage was never good to begin with.
> Doug came from a real poor background and
> was really into the macho trip. He wouldn't
> even let me hold his hand in the grocery
> store. He had a violent temper and would
> beat me when he had been drinking. One day

I came home sick from work and caught him
in _our_ bed with another woman. That was it.
I went to a lawyer and filed for a divorce
that day.
                    -Janis, 35, third marriage.

I knew I wasn't happy but we never fought.
He was such a shrewd politician that he
would make circles around my arguments.
He would always end up right and I would
end up thinking I was wrong. One day I
finally had had enough. I confronted him.
Do you or don't you love me? He admitted
that I was third in his life after politics
and Demolay. I couldn't live as being
only third in his life so I told him I
supposed we had better call it off. He
got out a yellow legal pad and divided
everything out and he left then. It was
over.
                    -Lisa, 32, divorced twice.

It appears that these women were willing to sub-
mit to long periods of unhappiness in a marital
arrangement as long as they felt that their husbands
somehow valued them above all else. For these
women, the quality of the marital relationship was
measured by their perceived importance in their
husbands' lives, not by the treatment they received
by their husbands. Some female multi-marriers sensed
shortly after marriage that their devotion to the
marriage and their respective spouses was not equally
matched by husbands. Some created situations in
which devotion to the wife could be evaluated.

Buddy and I had been married for about
three months when one night a bunch of us
went out drinking. We were all pretty
tight and somehow we ended up sleeping in
the same bed with my girlfriend. Someone
said something about Buddy and my girlfriend getting together. Buddy asked me if
it would be alright and I said ok. So
they had sex right then and there. The
next morning I left.
                    -Angela, 33, third marriage.

"Why did you agree to this if it would cause you
to leave?"

My daddy ran around on my mother so I
needed to see if Buddy would do it to
me too. I tested him--severe test--but
I needed to know if he really cared about
me the way he should. I needed to know
that I would be the only one in his life.
I wasn't so I left.

Female multi-marriers inserted so much "self"
into the marriage that they were willing to overcome
all obstacles to remain in the marriage with the
exception of one. They could not tolerate a marital
relationship in which the exchange of devotion was not
equal. Adjustment to the husband was expected and to
a large degree actually accomplished. It was only at
the time that they perceived they were not truly
loved by their spouses, did not come first in his
life as he did in theirs, was the decision to divorce
finalized and acted upon.

Unlike male multi-marriers who needed many
separations to finally complete the act of ending the
first marriage, women did not participate in long
drawn out separations. Once the evidence of non-
equality of devotion was presented and evaluated,
wives left their husbands with very few even considering a separation. If the husband did not love them
totally in the manner they felt necessary for the
continuance of the marriage, then the marriage was
effectively over and done with and only the legal
procedures remained.

Sure, I was unhappy for a long time with
him. He would put me down and sometimes
hit me when we were alone at home. I
decided to divorce him one night when we
were out at a bar with friends drinking.
Before, when we would fight he would make
up and say he loved me and I would accept
that. But that night he picked a fight
with me in front of the other people and
called me names. That was it. If he really
loved me he wouldn't treat me like that in
public. I threw a beer in his face and
left. We didn't actually get a divorce
for several months later but the marriage
was finished at that time.
                    -Lois, 27, divorced three times.

86

The day I left him he had been gone with
the guys hunting. He came home and they
all wanted supper. He said, 'Go fix
supper for me, bitch.' And that was that.
If he cared so little for me that he would
act that way in front of his buddies, I
wasn't staying. I put on my coat and left
and the next day filed for divorce.
                    -Meg, 39, divorced five times.

We had decided to separate to give him time
to think it all out. I wanted him to really
want me. I wasn't thinking about divorce
at that time. I just wanted him to come to
realize what our marriage meant. We decided
to get back together so we went to my parents
house for the weekend. He went out drinking
with a friend of his and didn't get to my
parents house until after three in the morning.
That was it--the marriage was finished. I
wanted a divorce.
                    -Janis, 30, third marriage.

Notice in each of these stories the social nature of
the decision to divorce. Each decision was made while
in the presence of persons other than the husband.
Even if the husband beat the female, argued with her
violently in the privacy of their own home, it was
still possible for the female to rationalize his
behavior and attributed it to her inability to adequately adjust to her husband. At the point the
marital relationship went public, so to speak, the
woman then realized that indeed her husband did not
truly care for her. Face, in Goffman's (1969) sense,
could no longer be maintained and the painful truth
of the travesty of marriage was immediately dealt with.

    Female multi-marriers were so tied to the social
nature of marriage, the essence of their identity
being derived from that marriage, that the decision
of divorce was preceded only by the social death of
the marital relationship. Marriage was no longer
conceived of as a joint act on the part of the two
partners involved. Only one, the female, was still
attempting to create a happy and successful marriage.
When the delusion of joint involvement was publicly
displayed as being false, the female reconciled herself to the loss of her marriage and subsequently
divorced. In essence a successful degradation
ceremony (Garfinkle, 1956) had occurred and female

multi-marriers discarded the damaged identity.

The Commonalities of First Marriages

for Males and Females

This chapter was written on the assumption that the first marriage and divorce was experientially different for males and females. However, there is one factor found in common in all the marriages discussed which, in and of itself, created hardship and interactional barriers for the participants. This one difficulty experienced jointly by male and female multi-marriers has to do with the problematic nature of social categories. Goffman (1963) explains the utilization of social categories as it applies to marriage in this way:

> In our society to speak of a woman as one's wife is to place this person in a category of which there can be only one current member, yet a category is nonetheless involved, and she is merely a member of it. Unique, historically entangled features are likely to tint the edges of our relationships to this person; still at the center is a full array of social standardized anticipations that we have regarding her conduct and nature as instance of the category, 'wife', for example, that she will look after the house, entertain our friends and be able to bear our children. She will be a good or a bad wife, and be this relative to standard expectations, ones that other husbands in our group have about their wives too . . . Thus whether we interact with strangers or intimates, we will find that the finger tips of society have reached bluntly into the contact, even here putting us in our place (p. 53).

So despite the fact that Udry (1966) suggests we have little knowledge concerning what actually occurs after the marriage ceremony, marriage is entered into with the firm understanding that to become married represents gaining membership into a new group or category. "To be married is to be placed in a special relationship to another person--a relationship whose boundaries have already been established and

88

whose general shape has already been determined"
(Udry, 1966, p. 23).

The problematic nature of social categories for
multi-marrieds lies within the overwhelming sense of
faith that males and females place in this belief
system. They each understand totally that marriage
implies a social reconstitution into a new classification, that of husband or wife. Unfortunately, as
it turns out, definitions of marriage, the meaning
of the social membership, is not congruent. For
males, accepting membership into the club of husbands
also means accepting marriage as drudgery. For wives,
happiness ever after is expected to be the result
of entry into the role of wife. Both men and women
share the understanding of the impact this new social
category will have on their lives; it is the meaning
applied to categorizing which is utilized separately.

Summary

Male and female multi-marriers entered into and
made decisions to leave the first marriage for
differing reasons. Males primarily married in response
to cultural directives in the form of pre-marital
pregnancies, pre-marital sexual activities, and peer
pressure in the form of expectations to marry.
Marriage was seldom thought of as a relationship
which would be personally enhancing. Females, on the
other hand, after years of being socialized into
viewing marriage as the tying of one's social identity
with a man, did enter the first marriage with high
expectations that such a venture would be personally
rewarding. Thus males and females entered into marriage with differing degrees of interest in marriage
as a joint action. Females expected to undergo
varying amounts of change in their lives while males
had considered the adjustment to marriage as only
requiring a slight, if any, degree of personal involvement.

For males, getting married, the act of marriage
itself, was sufficient response to social pressures
to marry. They had fulfilled role obligations and
considered themselves as having graduated into adult
status. For females, it was the routinized attempt
to put together an ongoing joint venture, the day to
day enactment of marriage, that was seen as the basis
for conceptualizing themselves as having achieved a
successful identity and consequently the transition

into adulthood. This point is seen most clearly in the differing responses to divorce. When asked to explain their feelings about themselves after the divorce was complete, men generally answered in ways which identified the finality of that chapter of their lives. "I just felt overwhelming relief" or "I felt like I had just been released from jail" were the usual variations offered. Women, on the other hand, were left with a sense of incompleteness and inadequacy. "I felt like a failure". "I felt like I was worthless. I couldn't keep my marriage together so what good was I?" Women, it appears, were stigmatized by the destruction of the first marriage. Men were not.

Having once been married, having responded to social pressures in the appropriate manner, men could continue to conceptualize themselves as inadequate persons. Women, stigmatized by divorce and feeling socially inadequte, were not able to sustain for themselves the notion of having successfully responded to societal demands.

Stein (1981) discusses the decisions to marry and divorce as being based on a series of pushes and pulls into and out of a particular situation. From Stein's perspective, pushes represent negative factors in a situation while pulls represent attractions to a potential situation. Utilizing this framework we can view male multi-marriers as having been pushed into the first marriage. To not marry, given the various circumstances of peer pressure, pre-marital pregnancy and sexual intercourse, would have resulted in their remaining in a situation which would have negative consequences. They entered into marriage to avoid these unpleasant responses, and not due to the inherent attractions marriage held for them.

Women entered into their first marriage due to the pulling effect marriage held for them. Having been socialized into acceptance of themselves as adequate individuals only upon marriage, then marriage can be seen as being an attractive solution for the completion of a joint and total social identity.

Decisions to divorce can also be viewed from Stein's perspective. Due to the public destruction of a joint social identity, female multi-marriers were pushed into divorce. Divorce held no attraction for

these women who so acutely felt the stigmatizing
nature of the act. Men, unhappy in the demands
placed upon them by marriage, were enticed into
divorce by the attractions of renewed bachelorhood.
Life was simply more fun at the pool hall, remember,
and while arranging for the post-divorce situation
of the wife was demanding and required skillful
maneuvering, still these individuals continued to
seek the freedom of the single life again.

Thus, again, just as in the social responses we
found to the commonalities of poor early childhoods,
males and females begin together the journey into
early marriage and divorce, each experiencing similar
situations in differential ways. Pre-marital
pregnancies, peer expectations, pre-marital sexual
involvements, and desires to enter into the status of
adulthood are processed and expressed in various ways,
with the commonality of response being defined by sex.

CHAPTER V

SECOND MARRIAGES: STARTING OVER

Introduction

In the previous chapter an understanding of the ways in which multi-marriers conceptualize marriage was presented. For men, marriage frequently was seen as a status conferring act and was entered into in response to role obligations. For females, marriage was perceived as having intense personal relationship to self and was sought as a means for creating a total social identity. For male multi-marriers divorce occurred when the weight of role obligations became too heavy. Female multi-marriers sought divorce in response to social stigma created by the public viewing of a defective marital relationship.

Divorce, for multi-marriers, should not be viewed as a rejection of marriage, but rather as representative of the high priority given to this relationship. These persons are so tied to the notion of marriage as the mechanism for interacting in society as capable and complete individuals that multi-marriers continue to seek marriage even after the somewhat traumatic destruction of their initial marital attempts. Attention is drawn then to the acute necessity of marriage as an identity-bestowing apparatus for these people.

In this sense, remarriage for multi-marriers can be discussed as an act which is undertaken in an attempt to rectify the sense of identity loss experienced through divorce. Weigert and Hasting (1977) in their discussion of identity loss within a familial context, suggest that divorce can be viewed as loss at the level of interactional and significant others.

> Such loss may be conceptualized as 'identity loss', the destruction or denial of a particular, meaningful, and positively affective self-other bond which has constituted a central personal identity for self. Identity refers to both a cognitive and an affective sense of a continuous and consistent self as socially situated by others' appraisals and personally projected onto others. It seems axiomatic that both personal existence and

92

social order require such a sense of identity (p. 117).

While personal existence and social order can be and most frequently are one in the same, in terms of multi-marriers, however, identity for male multi-marriers implies a concentration on the requirements for social order which are generated by marriage. Female multi-marriers, on the other hand, are concerned with the totality of marriage as personal existence. In this sense then, divorce can be seen as identity loss and remarriage may be viewed as an opportunity to regain a sense of identity for multi-marriers as a whole.

Often the dissolution of the first marriage with its inherent aspects of identity loss is presented in popular literature as an analogy to death. Divorce is seen as creating social death. Given this particular bonding of divorce with death, many family writers advocate a certain cooling period after divorce. A grief and mourning period is recommended and it is felt that the individual needs some time alone in order to restore a sense of balance (Waller, 1930; Hunt and Hunt, 1977; Weiss, 1975; Westoff, 1975).

The conceptualization of divorce as social death may indeed be quite valid for multi-marriers, at least in terms of the interactional barriers created for a good portion of them by divorce (Brandwein, 1974; Goode, 1956). However, little evidence is seen which indicates that these individuals undergo any extensive mourning and grief period at all. Very little, if any, time is spent in reflecting on the history of the first marital relationship. Multi-marriers do not concentrate on gaining insight into the problems which plagued their first marriages. The past is put behind them and all energy is centered on future relationships. In short, bridges are burned and no lessons are learned.

Like the Phoenix, these individuals arise from their own ashes and rapidly seek out new relationships. They remarry in very short order. The average time spent single between the first and second marriage is 13 months. Male multi-marriers have generally remarried within 11 months while females take slightly longer and remarry within 14 months. For over 80 percent of these persons, the marriage does not mark the beginning of the new intensive relationship. Most of

93

these individuals had left first spouses and were
living with future spouses within three to four
months. Very little time is actually spent alone
without engaging in a heterosexual relationship.
New relationships are sought as soon as the old are
dead, often without allowing time for the "body to
become cold".

Considering the rapidity with which multi-marriers
engage in new relationships, one is left with the
conclusion that multi-marriers are individuals who
are strongly drawn to marriage and dyadic relationships. In exploring the remarriage and subsequent
divorce experience of multi-marriers, there begins to
emerge a focus on remarriage as an attempt to restore
social order and regain identity loss. The behavior
evidenced by many multi-marriers appear to establish
credibility for Goode's (1956) conclusion that
remarriage represents a solution to the ambiguous
status of being divorced. Hunt (1966) also noted that
many divorced persons do not consider themselves wholly
successful until they remarry. Additionally, as
Bernard points out (1956), contemporary community
attitudes appear to be receptive toward remarriage
for the divorced. However, as we progress through
the course of the biography relating remarriage
experiences, there appears a new element. For some,
the meaning of marriage becomes altered as the
individual incorporates interactional skills with past
experience.

Given the fact that initial marriage and divorce
impacts differently on males and females due to
differential perceptions of social phenomenon, it
should hold true that remarriage and divorce, as
experienced by multi-marriers, falls also within
this pattern. "His" and "her" construction of reality
as they pertain to second marriages are evidenced by
both males and females as they relate their life experiences. Meanings emerge and are utilized differentially by each sex, congruently, biographical histories
of remarriage are also offered to the reader as a
function of this differential processing of reality.

In short, males and females continue to share
common life experiences but each similar episode is
interpreted differently.

Starting Over: The Feminine Way

Divorce as a Failure

For the female, the first divorce represents a sense of failure as a person. These are women who have been socialized into expecting the marriage relationship to fulfill their lives, to create the cement which binds together for them a social identity. When divorce occurs, these women are left with a fragmented social identity, an incompleteness of self which evidents itself in overwhelming feelings of inadequacy. As Kraus (1979, p. 115) points out, "an individual whose value system says that a divorced person is a failure, and a person without a mate is worthless, will most certainly experience a great deal of distress if he finds himself in that position".

> I felt like such a failure. I had gotten married because that was what a girl was suppose to do. I waited on him hand and foot because that was what a wife was suppose to do. When I got divorced I didn't know what to do, I didn't know what I was suppose to do. I only knew that I didn't do what I was supposed to do--that was stay married.
>
> —Angela, 33, 3rd marriage.

> After my divorce and I was on my own I didn't know what to do. I needed to know that men would find me attractive. I needed to be validated as a woman. I didn't think anyone would ever want me again.
>
> —Frieda, 35, divorced three times.

All too often these feelings of inadequacy are expressed as fears concerning their ability to function alone, devoid of a man in their lives.

> After the divorce I was so afraid. I was afraid to date and I had never lived alone before in my life. I was afraid to go out of my house at night. I felt like a single woman living alone was asking for it. I kept all the lights on in the house all night long and I wouldn't answer my phone if it rang after dark. I was terrified of being by myself.
>
> —Jean, 27, divorced twice.

95

Others expressed their fears of inadequacies behind
a front of bravado.

> After my divorce I got real tough. I
> figured men wouldn't want to go out with
> someone who was divorced so I figured I
> had better learn to make it on my own. I
> didn't think anyone would ever look after
> me again so I would make myself be strong
> and look after myself. I told myself I
> <u>could</u> and <u>would</u> learn to not let the mechanic
> take me on car repairs just because I was
> a woman. I just got tough.
> > -Sheila, 29, divorced three times.

Despite fears for the future and strong feelings
of inadequacy, none of these women ever seriously
considered returning to the ex-spouse. The old
marriage was not seen as a cure for the sense of failure these women were experiencing.

> I felt real low after the divorce. I was
> disappointed in myself. I kept thinking
> if I had only been stronger, had only put
> up with him more or been more tolerant. I
> felt like I had failed somehow. I felt like
> it was my fault because I wasn't good enough.
> > -Lois, 27, divorced three times.

"If you felt this way, why didn't you consider going
back with your husband?"

> No, no. I knew that marriage was over and
> I couldn't, didn't want to go back. I just
> felt that maybe if I were a better person
> it wouldn't have happened the way it did.
> I knew it (the divorce) wasn't my fault
> but I felt like it was. I didn't want to go
> back because nothing would change but I
> felt like it was my fault.

For this woman, like so many others, her sense of
identity had hinged on being married. To fail at a
marriage no matter how great the justification was
internalized as a failure. Each understood that her
divorce was necessary and that to return to the
marriage would not be wise, however, each conceptualized themselves as having somehow been responsible
for the shattering of a dream. This sense of
responsibility for failure was seen over and over
even as women told of husbands' beating them.

> When he first beat me I guess I felt like
> it was my fault. I guess I deserve it.
>   -Janis, 35, third marriage.

Thus, when the marriage ended, sometimes due to
repeated beatings females continued to experience a
sense of failure because they had not accepted the
beatings, although intellectually they realized this
punishment was not deserved.

Remarriage as Emotional and Financial Security

This sense of failure and inadequacy often
combined to create social pressure which pushed the
newly divorced woman into another relationship. Most
tell of meeting their second husbands shortly after
the first divorce and rushing into another marriage.

> I was a student in Peds and he was the
> resident. He called me at home and told
> me he was going through a divorce. I
> understood how hard that could be and went
> out with him. Only later did I find out he
> was just separated and not divorced. By
> then it was too late. . . We were living
> together and I told him to get a divorce
> or get out of my life. So he filed.
>   -Lisa, 32, divorced twice.

"If you didn't want to date a married man, why did
you continue to see him when you found out he was
still married?"

> I like fixing breakfast for a man. I like
> going out with a man and knowing that I am
> with him. I just don't see how you can be
> happy without being married. Marriage is
> your adult fulfillment. I wanted to be
> married and I was in love with him by then.
> We were having sex and it bothers me to have
> a sexual relationship with someone I am
> not married to. Besides, do you have any
> idea what it is like to be my age and try
> to find available men? Most men wouldn't
> even talk to me when they found out I was
> a doctor.

"Being a doctor isn't enough?"

> I am an independent person and I can do any-
> thing I want but I like having someone, a

man, have his arms around me. I need that, despite everything else I have, I need that too.

Most multi-married females tell of marrying for the second time in order to secure for themselves some aspect of feminity which was missing.

> I met my second husband shortly after my divorce and he moved in with me soon after. We lived together for three months before we got married. I wanted children so I married him to have children. We got along alright so I figured why not get married.
> -Patty, 30, third marriage.

> I had been doing a lot of partying and one night I met the most gorgeous man I had ever seen. I was convinced that if I didn't marry him no one would ever want me again. I felt lucky he was paying attention to me. I wanted so badly for us to be a family. I wanted another family so badly. I wanted a father for my son and I wanted to be a wife again.
> -Frieda, 35, divorced three times.

For others, the drawing attraction to marriage lay in the financial security such a relationship would make available.

> After my divorce I met this man I dated for about a year. We broke up even though I cared a lot for him. I moved to another town and met this CPA. He made lots of money. I could have everything I ever wanted. Money, clothes, go to school. So I married him.
> -Lois, 27, divorced three times.

> I was living with my grandparents because I couldn't make it alone financially. Doug wasn't paying any child support. I met this policeman and everyone kept telling me I should get married. My grandparents kept telling me I could have my own home and a father for my daughter. So I married him.
> -Janis, 35, third marriage.

98

Female multi-marriers entered second marriages for a variety of reasons. Most were pushed into remarriage by attempts to salvage fragments of self-conception. Others simply capitulated to the harsh reality of living alone and financial insecurity.

The White Knight Redefined

When discussing characteristics of the first husband which aided in the decision to marry, most females generally made some reference to an emotional attachment they felt for the husband. Most stated that they had been in love when they married. Curiously, few of these women made reference to love as the motivating factor for remarriage. With few exceptions, love is mentioned only as an after-thought.

"Why did you marry this man?"

Well, he wasn't as smart as my first husband. He didn't seem as intelligent but he was nicer. He seemed like he would be successful. I thought he would make a good husband.
                              -Jean, 27.

He was a better looking man than I was a woman. I think I married him because I thought he was my last chance.
                              -Frieda, 35.

I kind of admired him. He was a strong person and always got his way. I admired that kind of strength.
                              -Sheila, 29.

I really don't know why I married him. We had this long distance phone relationship and I guess I kind of just got caught up in it. I was so tired of being alone then and I wanted to be married. I had been working and he said he wanted me to stay at home and that sounded real good at the time. So I married him.
                              -Martha, 26.

He always said the night he met me he fell instantly in love with me. He was just so sweet and kind and good. We lived together for a year and then he said either marry me or I am leaving. I didn't want him to leave so I married him.

-Angela, 33.

I liked him and he was real involved with
his career. I figured I would be pretty
well left alone. I would be married, have
everything I needed in terms of money and
would be left alone for the most part. So
I married him. He was a nice man.

-Lois, 27.

The second marriage, it appears, is not necessarily a marriage which is based on love. With one exception, none of these women remember themselves as being
really in love at the time of marriage. Compared to
emotional responses elicited by the first husbands, it
would seem these women entered into second marriages
for more rational reasons; to provide a home for
themselves and their children, to gain financial
security, to simply be married again, and not for the
romantic notions which characterized first marriages.
Weigert and Hasting (1977) have predicted this
response as the possible result from previous painful
identity loss due to family disruption.

One strategy may be pursued which involves
the redefinition of the family as constituted
by more universalistic and rationalized
relationships. Marriage may be defined on
a rational, utilitarian, autonomous, and
purely contractural basis. The construction
of marriage . . . as such may allow the
contracting parties to avoid the experience
of particularistic identity loss with respect
to the spouse (p. 1182).

The attempt to become more realistic or rational
towards marriage can be evidenced in the qualities
sought in a new husband. Women looked for men who
were nice, potentially successful, or had a set
amount of money and these qualities superceded
romantic notions of love.

Interestingly enough, in terms of meeting social
identity needs, female multi-marriers married both
times for the same reason, that is, to establish selfhood in marriage. The difference lies in the explanation given for marriage by these respondents. These
women perceived themselves as having engaged in an
analysis of past marriages and decided that this new

marriage would be more practical. They set aside what they considered immature vocabulary of motives, that is love, and choose instead to concentrate on marriage as a utilitarian tool. Marriage became a practical endeavor.

In short female multi-marriers entered into second marriages with altered expectations. Marriage was no longer conceptualized as living in never-never land with "Prince Charming". Marriage instead was seen as a means to secure a desired lifestyle. Having been hurt by the magic of romantic love, these women were no longer willing to partake of the hair of the dog that bit them. Love was out, practicality was in. Marriage was the ultimate goal. A man was needed to secure that desired marriage and tape up fractured egos. The man no longer needed to be wonderful, he only needed to be nice and potentially successful. The need to tie oneself to a man was still the generating motivation for remarriage, however, the criteria for being the man had lessened. White knights no longer needed to be perfect.

The Disenchantment of Second Marriages

Considering the fact that these women entered into second marriages rapidly with altered expectations concerning the romantic nature of the marital relationship, it is interesting to note the enactments of these practical marriages.

"What was this second marriage like?"

Jerry was always going out with other women, even from the very first. I soon realized that he had only married me so he would be able to have his daughter with him.
                                    -Janis, 35.

After a while I began to see that he had only married me because of my financial support. He wanted to go to college but couldn't on his own. I had some money saved and I could work to support him.
                                    -Frieda, 35.

I had thought I would love being at home, not working and seeing a lot of the country. I didn't. I went crazy staying at home. He wouldn't settle down to one job so we

101

moved all the time. I hated living in
motels. He thought it was all in my head.
I thought it was too because I thought that
that was what I wanted. And when it wasn't
I figured I had to be crazy.
                              -Martha, 26.

We lived together for a year before we married.
After we married we started fighting. Suddenly
we no longer trusted each other. We had a
love-hate relationship. I don't understand
it. I had no reservations about marrying
him because the year we lived together was
not bad. I don't understand what happened.
                              -Sheila, 29.

And still, from the diary of a woman who wanted
to create a new family, secure a father for her son:

Jim is a good father to Jay and Jay is
already a daddy's boy. It makes me happy
to see them play together and do things
together. Jim is the only one who can
feed Jay with any degree of success. With
all the happiness I see between Jay and
Jim there seems to be something missing
between Jim and myself. It makes me so unhappy I want to die. It seems to me there
is no closeness between us concerning things
that touch a person's heart. The only thing
of immense value that we share is Jay. I
feel like I've failed completely as a wife.
                              -Frieda, 35.

Second marriages for these women represented a second
chance at securing a concept of self. The White
Knight had been redefined and these women had entered
into second marriages with an expectation of success
given the transformation of requirements regarding
mates. However, these marriages also ended in what
they perceived as failure and so anomie was intensified. Notice that the meaning of marriage, inasmuch
as it implies happiness ever after with one mate had
not been altered. Marriage, as a medium for securing
a social self, still reigns. Having redefined the
White Knight on a more practical basis, these women
were subjected to confusion and dismay when the
remarriages failed. Most regard the dissolution of
of the second marriage with ambivalence and for many,
years later, nagging questions still remain.

I don't know what happened to it. I was
so sure this one was right.
                              -Sheila, 29.

I just don't understand it. I thought
this time I would be married for life.
                              -Jean, 29.

It didn't make any sense. I did everything
right and it still fell apart. Even today
I don't know what went wrong.
                              -Lisa, 32.

Renewed Adjustments to Husbands

     For a period of time beginning with the first
realization that their marriage was on shaky ground,
these women often endured extreme measures in an
attempt to stabilize a rocky marriage. Attempts to
adjust to their husbands were often heroic.

     When we first got married we had agreed to
     live equal distance from our work. We would
     both commute equally. But he found a house
     which required me to drive almost two hours
     a day to my work. I didn't want to do it.
     But soon I realized he was going to live
     there with me or without me and I was trying
     so hard to make that marriage work I did it.
     He drove ten minutes to his work and I drove
     two hours for over a year.
                         -Lisa, 32, pediatrician.

     I just knew in my heart he was seeing other
     women. He denied it but I knew it anyway.
     I didn't want to admit it. He had me con-
     vinced that the reason we didn't have sex
     frequently was because I was a nympho. I
     was crazy and wanted it all the time. He
     was normal. Normal hell, he was just too
     tired from other women to take care of me.
     But I let him send me to a psychiatrist
     anyway to "cure" me of being a nympho.
     At that stage I was willing to do anything
     to keep things together.
                              -Frieda, 35.

     My second husband was just like my father.
     He broke my nose, he broke my arm. The
     marriage was going so bad. I fell into

the trap so many women do. I had a baby.
I thought that would straighten things up.
Even when he beat me up and the police
came in, I couldn't arrest him. If he was
in jail we could never work things out.
                                    -Patty, 30.

In the first marriage the social nature of information relating to the deterioration of the marital
relationship created the impetus for divorce for
these women. But by the second marriage, so tied to
the concept of marriage are they that even public
knowledge of the state of the marriage is not sufficient grounds for divorce. Others are allowed glimpses
of the marriage and still the marriage continues.
Neither policemen or psychiatrists are sufficient
grounds for dissolving the marriage.

The Second Divorce: Intensified Anomie or

Impetus for Change

Despite the intense desire to remain married in
the face of potent obstacles, divorce did occur. Most
marriages ended on the average within three years.
For half of these women, divorce was never seen as an
answer to poor marital relationships and finally it
was the husband who left the family over the protest
of the wife.

I finally filed. I didn't want to but he
wasn't staying and there wasn't anything
left that I could do.
                                    -Jean, 27.

The military sent him to Germany and he was
suppose to send for us when he found housing.
I never heard from him for almost a year.
I finally went to the JAG office and they
had him get in contact with me. It was
obvious he didn't want us with him and he
didn't want me. He told me to get a
divorce. There was nothing I could do. He
was over there and I was over here so I
finally agreed to it.
                                    -Frieda, 35.

From the very beginning things were bad.
But I wanted a child. I was already
divorced once and had no children. He
had children from a previous marriage and

didn't want any more. But I did and I
thought once the baby was here he would
change. He didn't . . . I finally asked
him if he was at all happy. He said no,
he didn't think he was meant to be married
and that we had better split. You can't
hold on to someone who doesn't want to be
with you so I had to let him go.
                                -Lisa, 32.

For a few women, the decision to leave the
marriage behind began slowly to germinate over a
lengthy period of time. Generally, for those women
who elected to divorce rather than those who were
left by husbands, divorce as an answer to a bad marital relationship began slowly as part of a process
which led to a questioning of their determined
acceptance of role conceptualizations. One young
woman described her decision to divorce her husband
as equivalent to having a veil lifted from her face.

If you are not married to that person, the
person can be nice to you, good to you.
It's easy if you are not married. When
the marriage started going bad I started
wondering why I was so unhappy, why I was
sitting up at night and crying. It finally
slowly began to sink in. I was the one who
had to do everything. We both worked and
I put in longer hours then he did yet I was
the one who did all the cooking and cleaning
and dish washing. He did nothing. It
slowly began to dawn on me that maybe that
was unfair. But it isn't all his fault.
He, and men, are the way they are because
women are the way we are. You spend the
first part of your life being influenced by
others. I was suppose to get married so I
did. I was suppose to have a baby so I did.
I was unhappy and I didn't understand why.
One night I realized that just because my
mother bought Rainbow bread doesn't mean I
have to buy Rainbow bread. Just because
she cut up my father's meat for him doesn't
mean I have to cut up my husband's meat.
It was like a flash of lightning hit me. I
didn't have to be unhappy because I was
doing everything I was suppose to. I could
change. Someone is suppose to take care of
me. Can I take care of me? I decided,

yes I can! I can take care of me and my
daughter and I can make it. One month
later I left him and I have never looked
back.
                              -Angela, 33.

Another describes her changing attitudes differently.

All I had ever wanted out of life was a
washer and dryer and six kids. I had
tried twice to make that dream come true.
When the second marriage started going bad
I finally realized that maybe I needed to
change my dream rather than just my husband.
                              -Martha, 26.

The realization that perhaps one needs to change
oneself, the intensity of the dependency on men or
the mindless repetition of social acts simply because
mother did them, comes to only a few women. Most
continue on in the understanding that if marriages
continue to fail, the fault must lie in the choice
of husbands, not in the manner in which marriage is
acted out on a day to day basis. Marriage is never
characterized as the villian. Only husbands are
seen as not contributing to the sustaining of mutually
constructed definition of reality. Frequently these
women judged themselves very harshly and attempt to
explain the failure of the second marriage as being
due to some inadequacy on their part. Note that it
is not marriage which is characterized as evil, when
blame is laid these women judge themselves, not
marriage.

I decided I was pretty rotten because any-
body that couldn't keep a man over somebody
that looked as ugly as Phyllis did.
                              -Meg, 39.

Today down deep I know that not all men
are assholes. However, I'm not willing
to put up with too much. I get bored
dating really straight men. I think my
next husband should be someone like my
step-father. He's intelligent and caring.
But nice men bore me. Is that a flaw in me?
                              -Martha, 26.

After two divorces I have to begin to
think that I am looking at the wrong kind

of guy. Why isn't marriage like Hart to
Hart (television program)? It just doesn't
seem like it should be that hard to get
along with someone if you work at it. Why
can't I pick the right kind of guys? If
I decide to think about marrying again I am
running to the nearest psychiatrist. I
want to know this time I haven't made another
poor choice.
                              -Lisa, 32.

What other people have in marriage is what
I want so it must be the men I choose to
marry.
                              -Sheila, 29.

   Over and over the theme is constantly replayed.
Marriage is not bad, some way, some how, the choice
of husbands is erroneous. It is as if the cliche
that hope springs eternal in the human heart is totally validated. These women advocate the belief that
successful marriage is dependent upon learning appropriate mate selection processes. These women still
strongly advocated the notion that lurking somewhere
out there, hidden behind some bushes or casually
eating breakfast at the local MacDonald's, is the perfect spouse. The White Knight in terms of being the
one man who can bring them total happiness in marriage
reigns and the quest is one of discovering the knight
who will make all dreams come true. One woman
describes this tendency on the part of female multi-
marriers concisely:

I feel like I am getting old and Mr. Right
better come along soon and announce himself
to me. I have wasted so much of my life
looking for Mr. Right. I want to share and
rely and trust in someone and I have not found
him yet.
                              -Jean, 27.

And so the search continues.

        The Quixotean Quist: Obstacles to Marriage

   Approximately half of the women interviewed
were presently divorced from their second husbands
and had not yet remarried. Most of these women were
engaged in some type of intensive relationship with a
man. All were ambivalent about the future of these

                    107

relationships. None felt secure with the knowledge that Mr. Right had been found. Despite the strong motivation and belief that this special someone needed to be discovered before attempting marriage again, most of these women were immobilized by fear. They remained in these not so perfect relationships for fear of either not finding Mr. Right or due to the sheer inability to gather strength for the quest.

> I hate to be alone so I would rather be married. Loneliness overrides what a person is really like. I have been living with Gene for over a year but I won't marry him because he is not good father material.
>   -Jean, 27.

> "But you say you want to get married again. Why are you living with someone who you feel you won't ever marry? Doesn't this prevent you from perhaps finding someone you would be willing to marry?"

> I guess so. But you don't understand. I am afraid of being alone. If I were to look for the right man I would have to leave Gene for now and then I would be alone. I guess I keep thinking maybe I'll run into him (Mr. Right) at TG&Y or the grocery store and then I won't have to be alone.

> Right now I'm dating the nicest man--so warm and kind. But I just don't love him. Why don't I fall in love with someone like him? Maybe I just ought to marry this guy and maybe it will work out. He's not <u>the</u> <u>one</u> but maybe he is close enough. I don't know. I know I won't marry him. I guess I should date around some but he's here. I stay busy with work and don't have the time really to party. He's not the perfect man for me but for the moment, he's the only game in town.
>   -Lisa, 32.

The search for the elusive mate is a never-ending cycle, beginning generally with the second husband and continuing on through three or four marriages.

> I got married five times because I had all

this hero ideal. You know, this is my
husband and everything is going to be
beautiful and we're going to live happily
ever after. Of course, that's the way it's
been every time I got married. It would
last maybe three months.

-Meg, 39.

And so they divorce after a might struggle to
somehow fit their husbands into the role of Mr. Right.
And when the square peg does not fit into the round
hole, the search is on again for the peg which will
fit perfectly. Only a few, a very lonely few, begin
to understand that perhaps it is their conceptualization of how marriage is to be enacted which should be
examined. Most continue on concentrating on the union
of the perfect man with the perfect marriage.

Their dismay and agony over the treacherous road
traveled to reach this goal creates incredible
feelings of inadequacy and incompetency. Every woman
interviewed displayed this sense of uncertainty and
insecurity. Each, in their own words, sought counsel
from the researcher. "You are the expert. You tell
what I am doing wrong." "Why do you think I am
choosing the wrong men?" Always, sadly, always, the
emphasis is on developing skills for identifying Mr.
Right. No one considered that perhaps the ways in
which they engaged in the practice of marriage should
be re-examined. The continual theme replays. Marriage
is right, it is simply the men whom they choose to
marry who create the deficit. "Show me how to
choose the right man and I will show you that I can
have a successful marriage."

The anomie intensifies. The first marriage,
based on some notion of love, is destroyed. The
second marriage, utilizing a more rational approach,
still fails to be consummated. The mythological
state of the perfect marriage with the right man fails
to materialize. The search continues, the Don Quixote
myth of wedded bliss lives on.

Starting Over: A Masculine Flair

Securing Positive Attributes Through Marriage

Male multi-marriers, like female counterparts,
are seldom alone for very long. They quickly form
new relationships immediately after the first divorce

and have usually remarried in very short order. Most remarriages for men, as for women, follow after a brief time of living together with the future spouse.

There appears to be several points of departure from the route taken by their female counterparts in terms of entering into a new marriage. Men have a tendency to conceptualize and describe these new spouses in more glowing terms than do female multi-marriers. With very few exceptions, male multi-marriers seldom referred to any physical attributes of beauty first wives possessed but yet some notion of physical attractiveness is always emphasized when attempting to explain rationale for entering into the second marriage.

> She was a good looking woman. I mean a _fine_ looking woman. She walked by my apartment one day and I turned to a buddy and said, 'See that fox. She is going to be my next wife.'
> > -Fred, 37, married three times.

> I fell for her the first time I went out with her. She was nothing short of beautiful. Big knock-out eyes and a super figure. She was the kind of woman that made other men turn around and stare.
> > -David, 30, divorced twice.

> This wife I really cared for. She was attractive, everything I had ever wanted in a woman. She was smart, pretty, an athlete and educated. A real winner in every sense of the word.
> > -Charles, 41, married three times.

Also considered in the assessment of the second wife are qualities found lacking in the first wife.

> She was so mature, bright and attractive. I respect her more than anything. I thought she would be good for me.
> > -Mark, divorced three times.

> My second wife was different. She was the more dominant, she was more of a leader. My father respected her where he didn't the first because she would stand up to him. I like a gutsy woman. She was confident.

Second marriages were entered into not through the social pressure of premarital pregnancy or intercourse and not because it was expected of them. Male multi-marriers conceptualized these marriages in terms which seem to imply that these wives were chosen on the basis of some personal qualities which these men admired. One is struck by the notion that attractiveness or intelligence was the criteria utilized for entry into remarriage. In describing these marriages men do not use words or phrases which connotate any sense of entrapment into marriage, which was often the case in the first marriage. Second marriages, then, were seen as having been entered into freely, devoid of the cloak of social coersion which so frequently characterized the bitterness of the first marriages.

Were second wives that much more attractive than first wives? Obviously, for the husbands they appeared to be. However, beauty is in the eyes of the beholder and perhaps certain social factors were at play which influenced perceptions of beauty. Given the emotional hardships encountered when leaving first marriages, a vocabulary of motives which justified such an act could diminish guilt felt over rejecting role obligations. To leave an ugly wife and a marriage of drudgery for the implied gaiety of bachelorhood could certainly be construed as the act of an irresponsible, immature person. However, to end an unpleasant marriage in order to secure for oneself a marriage of happiness with an attractive partner, given societal concerns today with finding personal fulfillment, would be more acceptable to an audience which advocates individual freedom, an audience of the "me first" generation.

Rebuilding Social Order by Remarriage

Another interesting aspect of second marriages which differentiated male and female multi-marriers is the element of timing. Most female multi-marriers remarried rapidly in order to be married again, to regain a lost lifestyle. Male multi-marriers appeared to have entered into second marriages in conjunction with an individual choice to alter their present lifestyles. Quite a few of these men married at a time during which they were also changing jobs or moving to new locations.

My second marriage was wham, bam. I met her, moved in with her within two months.

I wanted to get out of town, to try some-
place new. I decided to move to New Mexico
and she wanted to go with me. So we got
married. I wanted a new beginning and she
wanted to go with me so we tried to do it
together.
                    -John, 39, divorced six times.

I had moved to Maryland. I thought I
would have a chance to start out big there.
I had moved hoping for a changed environment
and making a whole new life. I was living
with her two weeks after I got to Maryland.
We had a lot of fun when we were living
together so I felt marriage would be part
of the change in my life too so we married.
                    -David, 30, divorced twice.

I was changing occupations at the time. I
wanted to get away from my father and I
thought I would change everything about
me. I thought we should start life anew
together.
                    -Mark, divorced three times.

Thus we see second marriages for males as somehow different from that which is experienced by
females. For men, marriage, due to the attractiveness of the new spouse is seen as an act which will
personally enhance them and will justify their previous reneging of social responsibilities. By
combining this new marriage with contemplated changes
in work and lifestyles, male multi-marriers are able
to achieve a renewed sense of social order in their
lives. Female multi-marriers, seeking more than the
restoration of simplicity in their lives, are driven
to regain a totality of self, the essence of social
life. Females remarry in order to obtain bread, the
sustenance of their existence. Men remarried in
order to treat themselves to the "icing on the cake",
so to speak.

Second Marriages: The Emergence of Dissillusionment

Considering the fact that these men entered
marriage on a more joyful note than the previous
time, it was often a painful experience to watch the
icing on the cake slowly melt away.

My marriage at first was terrific, just

terrific. I can't say enough about it . . .
After a time we were so busy that we just
stopped building feelings for each other. It
was a marriage of convenience. God, it was
sad to see that beautiful woman turn away
from me.
                              -Mark, 36.

I married that good-looking woman. I
wanted her to be mine. But the marriage
only lasted a month. She had two kids
and she was very lax in discipline. The
little shits were always running around
and getting into everything. I just
couldn't handle that.
                              -Fred, 37.

She was so beautiful and so young. But
she wanted to stay young forever. I
wanted to settle down and create a home
but she wanted to still run around and
party.
                              -Jeff, 37.

I went to New Mexico because I wanted a
clean break, a fresh start. The only
recreation in that place was the bars
and she didn't like the bar scene. So
I kept on going by myself and we just
drifted apart.
                              -John, 39.

At first it was great - everything was
perfect. Then I found out she was having
an affair. The deception and the trickery,
the betrayal I couldn't cope with.
                              -David, 30.

Bitterly these men discovered that the new marriage
was not destined to remain the sweet concoction they
had envisioned. Somehow these younger, more attractive new wives were scarcely different from the first.
These wives, just like their first wives, also had
expectations of marriage which clashed with theirs.
This created a phase of confusion for these men.
They had little understanding of why the dream ended in
the harsh reality of another divorce. For some, the
ending was preceded by actions performed by their wives
which stressed the dicotomy of each different set of
expectations. Some men wanted to "settle down and

create a home" only to discover their wives were interested in careers or a lively lifestyle of parties. Others expected the marriage to be a continuation of the fun experienced while living together only to discover that being married created a desire in the wife to settle down. Others, after engaging in extra-marital activities during the first marriage, were amazed to find that women also engaged in that type of behavior. Again, as in the first marriages, men were dismayed to find that these new wives were not capable of adjusting to the husband's demands, no matter how varied or lessened from demands imposed on previous wives.

Embryonic Attempts At Change

To a certain degree one is left with a feeling that some of these men did attempt to accomodate their wives in order to stabilize a rocky marriage.

> We were married for eight years. During that time I changed away from what she liked. I gave up football coaching and the lifestyle of jock to go back to graduate school. She didn't like where we were living or how we were living. I told her to go find what she wanted to do and where she wanted to live. She did that. I thought she would be back and be more satisfied with me after a while but she never came back.
> -Charles, 41.

> When I came back from summer camp she told me she was unhappy and needed time to herself to discover herself. I agreed that she could go and do that. I thought it would be good for her and she would return refreshed, ready to try all over again. I was wrong. She never returned and instead filed for divorce.
> -Mark, 36.

What we appear to be seeing in some of these men is an attempt to bridge their individual expectations of marriage and marital behavior in order to reach out to the unhappy wife. If she needs to get away for a while, alright, she can go. On the surface it would seem that perhaps these men have begun to alter conceptualizations of marriage, have begun to exhibit

114

more flexibility. However, under deeper questioning,
one still can glimpse a view of the rigid, stero-
typical pattern of behavior manifested by these men
since early childhood.

"You say the marriage was always terrific but
yet your wife left."

The marriage was terrific. Her leaving was
something she had to do for her. It wasn't
necessarily the marriage.
                                        -Mark, 36.

"When you realized she wasn't coming back, did
you attempt to talk with her about this?"

Even though we were very close, a great deal
of sharing, we never really talked about
any problems.

"Why not?"

There was never a real need to. I could
pick up from her when something was wrong.
If I figured out what was wrong, I changed
it. If I couldn't, over time it generally
went away on its own.

In short, what we see occuring is the internalization
of a new vocabulary which could be used to indicate
a less structured role pattern, although in actuality
the behavior of these men demonstrates an incon-
gruency between vocabulary and behavior.

Divorce as a Learning Experience

For other men, attempts to restructure the relationships never occured and divorce was quickly
centered on as the answer to a bad relationship.

As I told you, the marriage only lasted a
month. The kids were more than I could
handle. I told her that this has just
started and it is going to be this way
forever and I can't handle it. I want out.
I told myself that I have done it once,
dammit, I can escape again. So I did.
                                        -Fred, 37.

I could see within the first two months

that this wasn't going to work out. So I
knew I could leave. After you have done it
once, it isn't so hard.
                                    -Tom, 39.

All the men talked with during this study spoke
of the relative ease with which they were able to
leave the second marriage as compared to the first.
All indicated that the actual process of dissolving a
marriage through divorce was easier the second time
around, at least in terms of coming to the decision
to leave and implementing that decision. As one man
explains it;

    It's like going to the dentist to have a
    molar removed. The first time it is hard,
    you don't know how much it is going to
    hurt. The second time you know how hard
    it will be, but you also know that you will
    survive the whole thing. Knowing that you
    will survive makes it easier.
                                    -Mark, 36.

Understanding that one does indeed survive a
divorce is no indication that one will be oblivious
to the social forces which define the position of a
twice divorced individual in this society. Whereas
in the first divorce these men experienced a certain
amount of guilt in terms of running out on role
obligations, the second divorce is less guilt producing
but far more traumatic in terms of social identity.
For the first time some of these men begin to question
personal qualities they possess or at least to explor-
ingly consider perhaps they may be deficit in some
manner.

    After two divorces you have to lose some
    confidence. I mean you begin to think
    what in the hell is wrong with me?
                                    -John, 39.

    After losing twice, I thought I had better
    stay single a while until I figured out
    what I was doing wrong.
                                    -Tom, 39.

What we appear to be seeing for a few males is the
tentative emergence of self in marriage. Having been
faced with two divorces, these men are beginning to
experience the same type of self-doubt so well known
to their female counterparts. The initial conceptual-

116

ization of marriage as representing some aspect of one's social identity is being formed, inasmuch as some anxiety is produced which creates a self image which is, for the first time, being questioned.

The Male Myth of Happy Marriages

However, for the vast majority of male multi-marriers, looking back generally does not occur often and most continue on in new relationships or marriages with very firm definitions of the situation which allows little freedom for introspection, but great flexibility in how they view themselves and their condition.

> People who marry a lot are people who are looking and one of these days they are going to find that something they are looking for with that someone they need.
> —Jeff, 37.

> No, I don't plan to marry for a third time but I might. If I do it will be something that will just happen and when it happens I will just know it's right. If circumstances were right and it felt right I would do it.
> —David, 30.

Good heavens, shades of the White Knight syndrome! Do these men really believe that marriages are made in heaven and one day they will stumble on to the perfect marriage? Apparently so. Those men who experienced little personal doubt after the second divorce have a tendency to conceptualize their previous two marriages as simply being something which was not meant to be. Again, as with female multi-marriers, there exists a tendency to explain away two marriages by referring to "wrong choices".

There is no indication that negotiation of marriage is a valid concept for these people and when the marriage ends, it is visualized as something which should never have occurred to begin with. We again see a belief that communication between spouses will not help relieve any tension within the marriage. If the spouse is not happy, there is little the husband can do. After all, her unhappiness is her problem, not his.

As with female multi-marriers, we see two tenuous groups of people emerging from male multi-marriers.

117

The first group considers the dissolution of the
second divorce as "one of those things". There is
little self-doubt experienced due to the belief that
out there somewhere exists the perfect spouse and
perfect marriage and, in time, one might be lucky
enough to encounter it. A few males begin to doubt
the dynamics of their interaction patterns and begin
to question their ability to adequately engage in
marital relationships. Perhaps, for these men, some
change occurs.

                         Summary

Second Marriages

     Second marriages appear to be very similar to
first marriages in many ways. There appears to be
scarcely any more negotiation of the marriage
experience this time as compared with the first time.
Spouses still do not talk to each other, either before
or after the marriage ceremony. Multi-marriers, after
an amazingly short courtship, enter the new marriage
with the same rigidly defined roles. There is no
increased flexibility with which to cushion the
experience of day to day living. Each proceeds on
the assumption that his own construction of what
constitutes a marriage is virtually identical to that
of his partner.

     It generally takes a much shorter amount of
time for the recognition of this marriage as being
not particularly good to emerge. For females this
understanding generates typically two types of
responses. Most begin a series of adjustments to
their husbands wishes and demands in an attempt to
stay the execution. The manuevers do not work and
women are left with increasing amounts of insecurity.
For a few females the second marriage creates an
environment which generates new insight into conceptualizations of self and role playing and we begin to
see a hint of altered ideology pertaining to marriage
and social identity.

     Most men enter the second marriage expecting it
to be an easy task, perhaps thinking that this time
around the whole situation will work out. When the
marriage falters, it is considered the luck of the
draw and perhaps next time the cards will be dealt
more justly. A very few number of men begin to
experience an episode of self-doubt which manifests

itself in feelings of inadequacy. For the most part
though, this marriage is entered into willingly and
when it ends, it is conceptualized as being the result of poor choices in mates, although it is generally some favorable attribute of the wife's which
initially drew the man into remarriage.

In short, what we are seeing is a reversal of
the positions which initially accounted for the first
marriages. In first marriages men considered themselves coerced into marriage. They were pushed into
the affair by the strength of social pressure. The
second marriage can be viewed as experiencially
different. Males willingly entered into this
marriage so thus it was attractions which pulled them
into the situation.

For females, the social situation of being
divorced and without a man was so unpleasant, so
alienating, that they were in essence pushed into
remarriage, for to remain single held no attraction.
Having once undergone the grueling social nature of
divorce, most of these women were willing to go to
further lengths in order to adjust to second husbands,
often in a futile attempt to ward off another divorce.

With limited exceptions, which will be discussed
more extensively in the next chapter, male and female
multi-marriers continue to conceptualize marriage
as a state of being. You either are married or you
are not. If the relationship remains good you stay
married and if it does not, you divorce. No one
appears to understand that marriage is a process
requiring negotiation throughout its entirety.
Marriage still remains a fixed image. The goal is to
attain that fixed state, even if the route to eventual
marital happiness requires changing partners many
times. Given enough times at bat, surely, eventually,
one will find the right peg to fit into the right
hole. The myth of marriages made in heaven and
consumated on earth continues on.

CHAPTER VI

MULTIPLE MARRIAGE: ALIENATION OR CHANGE

Introduction

Many family sociologists, during attempts to
investigate the process of divorce, have chosen to
conceptualize divorce as a situation which requires
progressive stages of adjustment (Herman, 1974; Weiss,
1975; Bohannan, 1970; Krantzler, 1973). Divorce is
viewed as a traumatic episode in one's life (Goode,
1956) which requires a concentration of efforts to
overcome social-psychological obstacles which
necessarily thwart the route to a renewed, normal lifestyle. Implied in this conceptualization of divorce
as an adjustment episode is the viewpoint that those
individuals who do not successfully follow the various
stages toward "health" never finally achieve the goal
of an integrated self within a social context. In
short, the process of divorce adjustment incorporates
a developmental task approach and those individuals
who do not eventually reach the goal phase of adjustment consequently go on to experience more remarriage
and divorce, in other words, have the tendency to
become multi-marriers.

The process of multiple marriage and multi-
marriers as individuals have provoked little research
but nevertheless have generated sufficient attention
to create the use of several tentative labels.
Bernard (1956) has referred to those who divorce and
remarry several times as divorce prone. Glick (1973)
also addresses the problem of the divorce prone while
Bohannan (1970) has attempted a connection between
multi-marriers and his concept of divorce chains.
With few exceptions, most of the labels utilized to
describe multi-marriers connotate some type of mal-
adjustment which is termed pathological. People who
divorce frequently are seen as somehow neurotic,
dysfunctioning, or mentally ill.

Divorce often is, and may mandatorally be, a
process of adjustment for individuals, and while those
individuals who remarry and divorce numerous times
may also manifest neurotic behavior, divorce does not
necessarily have to be a situation which emphasizes
and further defines pathology. Kraus (1979) has
suggested that divorce should be studied for its

positive attributes rather than continuing on in the current tradition of conceiving divorce as disaster. A divorce, or several divorces may be viewed as a situation which provides an impedus for symbolic alteration and perceptual change. For the multi-marrier, divorce may be personally enhancing in terms of the incorporation of new interactional skills and may not necessarily indicate an individual who has become stalled at a particular developmental stage. What may occur is not an adjustment to the old pre-marriage social situation of being without the sig-nificant "other", but rather the creation of an environment in which the "other" is transformed in terms of meeting identity needs for multi-marriers.

While the final results of divorce can be viewed positively, the groundwork leading up to the decision to divorce can be seen as a crisis time in an individ-ual's life. It is during this time frame that many individuals must come to terms with the understanding that another attempt to secure an intensive relation-ship has failed. Often these people begin to examine certain attributes they feel they may or may not possess which are deemed responsible for yet another divorce. For multi-marriers, whose concentration in marital relationships is on its identity bestowing qualities, divorce may represent a true identity crisis. Stryker (1959) has suggested that the study of crisis within a family research context would prove most fruitful. As he states, "Crises will always threaten identifications, for the latter depend on stable activities of others with reference to one-self; and crises are likely to be important in the processes by which identities change" (p. 111). Multi-marriers, through the crisis of divorce, have lost certain characteristics of identity. The "other" is gone and for many there is a tendency to rapidly acquire another "other" with which to re-enact marriage. However, for some, the crisis situation which accounts for identity instability through loss of the "other" may also stimulate an introspection which aids in the creation and incorporation of new ways of managing aspects of social identity. The importance of the "other" may be transformed and the symbolic meaning of marriage becomes altered at least in terms of the usage of the "other" as the foundation for identity. Some researchers (Brown, Feldberg, Fox and Kohen, 1976) suggest that divorce aids in the creation of new identity attributes inasmuch as the respondents in their research associated the divorce experience with an increased sense of personal autonomy, a new sense of competence and control, development of better relationships with children and the freedom of time to develop their own interests.

Divorce, then, for multi-marriers, can be an experience which offers options. Some multi-marriers may utilize another divorce as a means for creating social change in their personal lives while, for yet another segment of multiple marriers, divorce is the instrument by which these individuals are further cast into the interactional behavior which reinforces the chances for another divorce. For the respondents in this study, it is possible to quite clearly see both options being chosen. As previously noted, multi-marriers have a tendency to become established in another marriage or intimate relationship immediately after the first divorce. However, at the conclusion of the second divorce, a trend begins to emerge which divides these individuals into two major groupings. Most multi-marriers, unable to feel secure without the identification of self in marriage, remarry rapidly for the third time. A small group of twice divorced persons, approximately one-fourth of the respondents, have elected to remain single for a period of time. These individuals have been single for at least two years and at the present time do not have any plans for immediate remarriage. Another small group of respondents are presently engaged in third marriages after spending an extensive period of time alone, often not remarrying after the second divorce for over four years. These individuals rate their present marriages as good and for the most part, these marriages have lasted longer than their second marriages did.

In essence, what has occurred is the formation of two major groups: those who remarried rapidly after the second divorce and those who either have not remarried or elected to wait several years before remarrying. A loose interpretation of the trend found among these two groups seems to indicate that those individuals who choose to remain single for extensive periods of time after the second divorce are more likely to enter into third marriages which they rate as relatively happy and stable. Those individuals who rushed into a third marriage after the second divorce are presently divorced from that marriage. For some of these individuals the process has continued throughout fourth, fifth, and even sixth marriages.

In looking at the data in terms of three or more divorces, time spent being single appears to become a cornerstone in understanding the process of multiple-marriage. Those individuals who are unable to perceive themselves as adequately functioning adults without marriage are the same individuals who continue to rush into marriages and subsequently experience numerous divorces. Individuals who utilize time as an element with which to undergo some type of personal change in terms of identity formation are individuals who have not remarried after the second divorce or waited several years before remarrying a third time.

As we follow the biographical history presented by multi-marriers, it appears that for those individuals who elected to remain single for a set period of time after divorce, time spent alone is conceptualized as an important element in what they perceive to be their own personal change. For those individuals who remarried quickly, time has no significant meaning. In essence, the second divorce is seen by the inter-actants as a real identity crisis. The ways in which multi-marriers choose to respond to this crisis in terms of valid social identity change or continued traditional identification patterns places these respondents in one of the two major categories.

Time as a mechanism for personal change is an attribute which can be found in its generic form among both male and female multi-marriers. However, despite the fact that multi-marriers of both sexes share in common the change potential found in time, for females this particular element assumes more crucial impor-tance. As with other socially derived perceptions, time is also conceptually defined differentially according to sex, and as such, is utilized in present-ing the biographies of multi-marriers.

The Feminine Response to Divorce Crisis:

Creation of Ambivalence

As we follow the biography of female multi-marriers throughout the course of two marriages and divorces, it becomes apparent that these are women who are caught in the throes of real anomie. They are disillusioned and discouraged. All they had been taught to have faith in, the American dream of wedded bliss, has proved to be erroneous for them. They are experiencing a real crisis in terms of identity.

Having been socialized into expecting identity to be derived from marriage, and having completed two unsuccessful attempts to fulfill a sense of self in marriage, the situation for many is perceived to be precarious. Anxiety is intensified as many of these women undergo a loss of faith in themselves and in their culturally derived aspirations.

Female multi-marriers were socialized to become, in a very real sense, the archetype of Riesman's (1950) other-directed person. For them, a sense of self is totally dependent on others for validation and the manifestation of successful integration of identity with marriage, has been denied them. Given their preoccupation with marriage as the measuring stick of self in association with poor past performance, there is little wonder that these are women who approach the concept of marriage with great amounts of ambivalence. They are drawn towards marriage by the nature of their identity needs while coincidingly are repelled by their own requirements.

Women who are divorced from the second marriage and are presently single, paradoxically approach marriage with a strong desire to remarry which is governed by a fear of marriage. Caught in a classical approach-avoidance conflict, marriage represents both the epitome of success and failure. Often, while discussing the possibility of future marriages, women expressed their confusion and dismay. Bewilderment is evidenced as women lash out at the betrayal by their own value system. The overwhelming desire to marry is held in check by a fear of being hurt by their own needs.

> Before I remarried again I would have a
> lobotomy to erase memories of how cruel
> people can be to each other when things
> take a turn for the worse, to erase how
> bad I can be.
> > -Jean, divorced for two years.

> I don't understand marriage. It just doesn't
> seem like it should be that hard to get along
> with someone. I'm just not sure what it takes
> to stay married.
> > -Lisa, divorced for 18 months.

> Today I think that deep down that not all
> men are ass holes so I do and I don't want

to get married again. I am scared of
marriage. I don't want to screw up again . . .
I just wish I wouldn't trust men anymore.
                    -Martha, divorced for two years.

A Need for Single Time: Problems and Benefits

During interviews these respondents all indicated
a need on their part to remain alone for a while,
hoping that a certain period of singleness would result
in gaining new knowledge and understanding with which
to take into a third, stable marriage.

One man, presently single for over eight years
after his second divorce, describes his reasons for
resisting marriage, a rationale utilized by all
respondents wishing to remain single for a while.

After two bad marriages I began to think
that perhaps there was something wrong with
me. I wanted marriage but I couldn't stay
married. I decided that I had better stay
unmarried until I had come to terms with
whatever was making marriage wrong for me.
I knew it wasn't fair to inflict my problems
on another marriage. First I work out all
my problems and then I get married again.
You just can't take individual problems into
a marriage, marriage has problems you have
to work on itself. It is defeating to be
dealing with individual problems and
together problems at the same time.
                    -Tom, 39, divorced twice.

However, the females divorced from their second
marriages, while attempting to follow the path laid
out by our male respondent are forced to combat social
forces which do not appear to be problematic for males.

Friday (1977), in commenting on the difficulties
facing women as they attempt to search for an identity
which is competent, complete and ultimately fulfilling,
often must overcome a powerful foe which has been
created for them by tradition and ingrained by
socialization.

We instill in them what psychiatrists call
a 'hidden agenda'. We say, Go to college,
succeed, be self sufficient, but we also
give them this message: If you don't succeed
as a wife and mother, you have failed (p. 183).

125

Female multi-marriers are women who were raised in an atmosphere which only emphasized the feminine, motherly nature of being female. Not having been encouraged to succeed at an occupation, to gain validation from any arena outside the home, to fail at the only avenue open to them for achieving a sense of self is an immense defeat. The inclination to rush back into another marriage is strong and to respond to an alien call to remain single for a while requires courage. Many of these women had not yet completed families and the desire to succeed as a woman, to have children, urges them into remarriage.

> I want to stay single until I am convinced
> I know what I am doing. But I also know
> that I'm getting old. Time is running out
> on me. I still have some miles left but I've
> wasted so much of my life. Soon I will be
> too old to have children.
> -Jean, 27, childless after two marriages.

> I already have one child but I would like
> to have another. The longer I stay single
> the less likely I am to have that child.
> That bothers me.
> -Lisa, 32, mother of one.

Relating directly to this notion of aging is the impact of a diminishing pool of eligibles. Women sense the scarcity of marriagable men and this increases anxiety to find a new mate.

> I know I probably shouldn't have married
> so soon but have you ever tried to find
> someone to even date at my age? I hate to
> use a cliche but a good man, at least a
> free man, is hard to find.
> -Lisa, 32, divorced from second husband.

> The only men still out there are bachelors,
> and that makes me suspicious. Why isn't he
> married? What's wrong with him? Or else
> they are divorced too and then you have all
> the problems involved with his ex. I know
> it's stupid considering the fact that I'm
> divorced twice, but you have to wonder
> what it is about the divorced man that
> made him get divorced? It's like, you
> know something is wrong with you, after all,
> you ended up divorced. But what's wrong

with him too? If you see a man who looks
like he's got it all together you have to
stand in line just to look at him.
            -Jean, 27, divorced two times.

Succumbing to the Double Standard of Aging

Men, more than women, are likely to remain single
for longer periods of time between the second and
third marriages. Males are simply not subject to the
same social pressures as females with regard to the
critical component of aging in this society. A great
deal of the desire to remarry experienced by these
presently single females was guided by the notion of
age in relationship to child bearing capacity. One
woman described her decision to remarry for a third
time to be the result of this aging component.

I always wanted one more child. The doctor
had given me one more year before I had to
have a hysterectomy. So I knew I either had
that child now or never. So I got married.
       -Patty, 30, mother of four children.

This notion of aging for women appears to play a
critical part in the decision to remarry for a third
time. Most of the females interviewed who were
presently engaged in or divorced from third marriages
indicated that in some way this concept of time taking
its toll influenced decisions to remarry.

"Why did you decide to marry for a third
time?"

Mike was so stable, a kind, caring person.
I thought he was the kind that would love
me til I died, you know, the real stuff. I
wasn't getting any younger. I also needed
a father for my son.
       -Sheila, discussing her third husband.

I was thirty-five years old and felt it
was time that I found a good, stable home
life. I felt the lessons I learned from
the first two marriages would combined
with the experiences I had had from just
living would make a third marriage good.
You would think that at my age I would
know more than I did when I was younger.
I felt like I was getting old quick and I

had better get my act together soon.
                    -Frieda, divorced from third husband.

As women grow older and are followed through the
course of two marriages, the concept of time as it
effects phases in one's life becomes an increasingly
important variable. Time becomes both an ally and the
enemy. For women who are divorced from second marriages, "single time" is often seen as the means by
which one comes to some understanding of the forces
which aided in the destruction of two marriages. Time
spent single is conceptualized as an asset in terms
of establishing successful male-female relationships.
Time is a respite, an occasion to be spent in self-
reflection. Time apart from marriage is a friendly
interval to be savored. However, operating jointly is
the notion that time is also the enemy. These women
become acutely aware of the ravages of time in terms
of the ability to have children, the aging process on
beauty, and the number of men available in a pool of
eligibles. Time is dual-faceted and few women are
able to overcome the concept of time as the enemy in
the end.

Those that fall prey to the notion of the ravages
of time remarry fairly rapidly, generally well within
a year from the second divorce and some within a
month or two. Those who remain single for several
years indicate that initially they had planned not to
remarry for a period of time but slowly they were
drawing near to the finality of time as the enemy. In
interviewing men, one is left with the impression that
time is seen only as an ally. Men do not fear aging
with the same sense of timing of life phases that
women possess. When men remarry quickly after the
second divorce, it is for other reasons rather than
a fear of being too old to bear children or find mates.

Third Husbands: A Process of Settling

For female multi-marriers, the dual pressures
created by the problematic nature of aging and a
diminishing pool of eligibles may result in a mate
selection process which is strongly influenced by a
sense of resignation. The notion of "single time" as
an aid in understanding the circumstances which
combined to create two divorces is tempered by the
knowledge that the passing time also results in a
lessened likelihood of obtaining a good man, one who
is untainted by previous divorces or interactional

problems of his own. Growing older and feeling a
sense of urgency in their search for self-fulfillment
in marriage, it may be difficult for these women to
uphold ideals which have already been tarnished. Ken
Kiser, family sociologist, has suggested that perhaps,
given the social pressures facing older women, female
multi-marriers are forced to settle on a man who can
provide certain tangible securities rather than
actively selecting a mate who may afford them the
opportunity of high levels of emotional involvement.
The notion of settling on a mate rather than actively
choosing a husband indicates a capitulation to a dismal future. When discussing motivations for remarriage, this idea of settling rather than choosing
appears to come into play.

Most females who remarry for the third time can
be seen as being pushed into marriage for a variety of
reasons, the most of which is the idea of time as an
enemy. However, other considerations are also evaluated. The ability of the future spouse to properly
provide financial security is a strong consideration.
While many of the females interviewed alluded to a
romantic feeling towards the third mate, all strongly
noted the importance of financial security as a
primary motivator for remarriage.

> Marriage means to me a stable home. Mike
> was able to provide that. I could stay at
> home and raise my child.
> > -Sheila, mother of one,
> > discussing her third husband.

> I wanted economic equality. He treats me
> as an equal and I contribute equally. I
> don't ever want to end up supporting a man
> again. He would never let that happen to
> him so I married him.
> > -Angela, remarking on third husband.

> I divorced my second husband because he
> wouldn't work and couldn't make any money.
> I want to be supported sometime too.
> > -Jean, divorced twice.

While some women did not list financial security as
part of the criteria for remarriage, the importance of
this factor is evident when women discuss reasons for
leaving the third marriage.

He had no initiative. He wouldn't get a
really good job and support us. He just
wanted to stay on drugs and keep jobs that
demanded very little. After three marriages
I had more goals than simply staying high on
dope.
   -Lois, 27, divorced from third husband.

I don't want to sound real material but he
just moved in here when we married. I
guess I resented the fact he brought nothing
financial into the marriage.
-Frieda, 35, explaining her third divorce.

Practicality reigns high again in terms of
motivation for third marriages. Women are looking
for stability, financial security, a family life and
all within a time framework. There is a sense of
urgency in the search for these qualities. Time is
running out and an adequate husband must be secured
soon. Few listed being in love as the rationale for
remarriage. Most internalized lessons from second
marriages and selected third spouses from men who are
different from troublesome second husbands.

This time I wanted someone who was not a
drinker. I didn't think at the time that
dope would be the same as alcohol.
     -Lois, discussing third husband.

He wasn't as good-looking as the second but
then, maybe he wouldn't chase the skirts as
much as the other one.
   -Frieda, discussing her third husband.

One woman, who had stated she married her second husband in order to secure an independent lifestyle,
reflects on the decision to marry her third husband:

I wanted someone to share everything with.
I had to share everything or I felt left
out. When I no longer was doing drugs and
he was, I wasn't sharing his life anymore
and we fell apart.
        -Lois, 27.

Another woman, after remaining single for six years
after her second divorce, describes with total honesty
her reason for marrying her third husband, a man ten
years younger than herself.

When you marry someone that much younger
than yourself, you can literally raise them
to be the way you want. You don't have to
be scared of getting hurt.
                              -Patty, age 30.

    Female multi-marriers marry for the third time
for the same underlying reasons which prompted earlier
marriages. The desire to establish selfhood in
marriage is still dominant, however, the social forces
associated with aging and a shrinking pool of eligibles
create additional burdens in terms of establishing
the quality of marital relationship desired. A third
husband does not necessarily need to be particularly
attractive or especially wealthy. Having undergone
considerable emotional trauma in terms of attempting
to adjust to the demands of second husbands, female
multi-marriers seek third husbands who will provide
them with a sense of security often judged missing
with prior husbands. In essence, these women look
for men who are not what they have married in the past.
They marry men who are not drinkers, not skirt chasers,
and who will not demand high levels of adjustment.
Often the attraction to third husbands is based not
on what these men are like but rather on what they
are not like in terms of the type of marital relationships these men seem to offer.

    One woman, Frieda, explains her third marriage in
this way:

    I had never had a Christian marriage before.
    I had other kinds but not this, so I figured
    why not?

Another, reflecting on the difference between her
present marriage and her second states:

    Sure, I got married again for security. I
    admit that. But this time it is different.
    He treats me as an equal person. I'm not
    dumb just because I am a female. We have
    mutual respect and for the first time for me
    in a marriage, friendship. This one doesn't
    expect me to wait on him hand and foot.
                              -Angela, 33.

The Effects of Single Time on Third Marriages

Many respondents, in relating the effects of single time, offered descriptions of themselves which reflected a renewed sense of self.

> I was petrified at the thought of actually buying a house all on my own. I had never bought before and here I was single with two kids and investing that much money. It was scary but thrilling all at the same time. I was finally doing something on my own.
> -Frieda, discussing her life after her second divorce.

> I finished college after that second divorce. I never knew if I had what it took to do it but I just knew I had to try to do something good for me, to make me feel good. I proved I was worth something when I graduated.
> -Lois, after her second divorce.

For the most part, single time was utilized by these females as a period to become equipped to deal more effectively with the world. Some completed educations, some bought houses, others accepted career advancements. Each secured some element of control in her life.

The effects of this newly established sense of control and autonomy can be ascertained by the types of marital relationships formed in third marriages. One woman, in attempting to describe the results of her single time, states the direct affect it had on her third marriage:

> I knew this marriage was going to be different from the first two. I had an education this time and knew I could take care of myself. If it didn't work out, I wouldn't lose everything this time.
> -Lois, after completing her college degree.

For those women who felt they had utilized their single time advantageously, there does appear to be a direct relationship between their sense of increased autonomy and what they perceive to be a better quality of marital relationship. For those women who were presently engaged in third marriages at the time of interviews and who rated those marriages as good, indicated that they were good because of the egalitarian aspect of the marital relationship. There is no evidence of the intensive adjustment to spouse which took place during the second marriage.

> This time I am a partner. This time I am
> not a doormat. This was my house that he
> moved into. I didn't move into his. We
> plan things together, not him making
> decisions and me carrying them out. We
> decide together and we do together--never
> again him deciding and me doing.
> -Angela, describing her third marriage.

> This marriage is good--better than the
> others. Tom changes diapers and feeds
> babies as often as I do. We both work and
> contribute money to the home. There isn't
> any more of my spending his money like in
> the first marriages. Now its our money--
> we both work for it. Tom does housework
> just like I do because he lives here too
> and dirties too. I guess the difference
> is it is our home, like our money. Being
> single for six years taught me the importance
> of having my own money and my own home. I
> would never go back to ever letting a man
> give me his money again.
> -Patty, describing her marriage
>   after single time.

For those women who had entered what they considered successful third marriages, single time was the one deciding factor which they felt had contributed to the establishment of a quality marital relationship. Single time had allowed them to develop a sense of control over their own lives and each took that sense of control and utilized it in creating a marriage relationship far different from the previous ones.

However, the confidence which resulted from single time did not always culminate in a happy third marriage. For a few of these women the birth of a sense of control only contributed to the destruction of the third marriage.

Those women who were divorced from their third marriages cited that in some ways this sense of control was responsible for the dissolution of the third marriage. A lack of willingness to adjust to new husbands created problems. One woman explained her third divorce in this way:

> He never understood why I left for work
> thirty minutes early. He didn't under-
> stand that I needed some time to myself
> before I started the day. He was jealous
> of any time I wasn't with him. I refused
> to be held accountable for every minute
> of my time away from him. When he said
> he thought it (the marriage) wouldn't
> work out because of all the jealousy, I
> agreed and left.
>
> > -Sheila, age 29.

Meg, 39, felt her marriage failed due to her unwilling-
ness to accommodate her husband. When he was trans-
fered to another state she refused to quit her job
and go with him.

> When the marriage started going wrong. I
> just left it. I wouldn't go with him. I
> had been through all that before and no
> way was I going to get left high and dry
> in another state. I loved him but I
> wouldn't do that again.

For some women it is the ability to control a
part of their lives for the first time which makes the
third marriage good. For others, it is a situation
in which one risks losing the newly established sense
of control which forces yet another divorce. These
women still seek marriage as a mechanism for establishing their credentials as wholly adequate females,
but yet, by the third marriage there is an assessment
of the price one has to pay for the successful creation
of that particular identity. Some find the price too
exorbitant and refuse to pay. Others succeed in
establishing a lifestyle with a new spouse which
affords them a certain amount of autonomy. By the
third marriage there exists a hesitancy to totally
absorb oneself into the marital relationship. There
is the beginning of a tendency to conceptualize self
as perhaps separate from a man. This realization that
perhaps one can stand alone, apart from a man, is
evidenced in the words spoken by a woman as she
describes the destruction of her third marriage.

Asking him to leave is the most courageous

thing I have ever done in my life. To tell
someone, a man, who loves me to leave me
because I am not happy took more courage
than anything I have ever done.
                              -Frieda, 35 years old.

This woman was amazed by her ability to put herself first, to leave the bonding with a man by choice.
She was impressed by her control over her own life. A
very heady first experience for her.

The slow emergence of control over one's life is
demonstrated in yet other ways also. Most of these
women underwent grueling first and second marriages,
often being the spouse left behind. By the third
marriage it is the female who does the leaving, and
often after a very short trial period. Several of
these third marriages lasted only a few months. There
appears to be little tolerance for lengthy adjustment
periods. It is assumed that if the marriage is to
work, it will connect immediately. If not, then it
is left behind rapidly.

Strategies for Identity Protection

By the third marriage female multi-marriers have
attempted to alter the importance of marriage. Having
undergone the traumatic experience of identity loss
through two previous divorces, they enact strategies
which will prevent total destruction. The most
frequently employed strategy is that of not investing
so much of "self". A part of "self" is held back.
Marriage has been defined by multi-marriers as identity
bestowing yet also pain rendering. Weigert and Hasting
(1977) have suggested that to the extent that moderns
foresee the probability of painful and meaningless
identity loss, they may seek to avoid its sources. As
Janis, age 35, explains her relationship with her
third husband,

I really trust Les. I don't think he will
hurt me. I know he would never hit me and
I don't think he will ever leave me. But
then, I thought that of my other husbands
too. I love Les and I know he loves me but
this time I'm not counting on it the way I
did before. This time I have my own career
and if it ends, it won't destroy me. I
give to Les as much as I can but I don't
expect him to hang the moon for me, I won't

let him be that needed. If he is still with
me in 20 years I'll let myself believe he
hangs the moon.

Female multi-marriers, having been socialized
into seeking identity through marriage, still continue
to do so. However, there is now a tendency not to
place all of one's eggs in a single basket. The
baskets have proven to be fragile in the past.

Another strategy utilized by female multi-marriers
during attempts to avoid pain is the alteration of the
meaning of marriage, at least as it applies to time
intervals. There is now little faith in the longevity
of marriage. Doubt is always present, even in those
third marriages which are rated by the participants as
good.

I don't know if the marriage will last.
He's 28 and has never been married before
and has never had any children. He says
it doesn't matter to him now but I know
that by 35 he might say to himself 'I'll
never have a child of my own'. You always
want to go into a marriage thinking it will
last forever but you are a damn fool if you
don't leave some options open. It would
crush you if you thought it would last forever.
                    -Angela, mother of one.

I guess I really expect him to leave when
he is 23 or 24. One day he is going to
think about all he missed out on by
marrying so young. He says he won't but
he will.
            -Patty, whose present husband was 18
                    at the time of marriage.

Expectations of marriage have altered. No longer
does anyone ask for forever. The emphasis is on now
and there is little future orientation in the third
marriage as women attempt to approach the relationship
more rationally.

My first marriage was an act of desperation.
The second marriage, well, that was hope,
that was maybe. With this third, I'm
comfortable, for now. I learned my lesson
with Johnny (2nd husband). I expected to
get gray and rock on the front porch with

that man. I thought love would conquer all.
Now I know better. Now I don't expect forever. Now I expect only for as long as it
lasts.

> -Patty, age 30.

The end results of the two major strategies employed by women during attempts to reduce threats to
a sense of self culminate in a self-fulfilling
prophecy. If one were to enter into a marriage not
expecting it to last, then should this not affect
the marriage? Perhaps the notion of marriage as being
a relationship which does not last works to insure
that it ends. By virtue of the creation of the
prophecy of eventual divorce, these women are further
motivated into not inserting a great deal of investment into the relationship. They have learned not to
care deeply for something which is transient.

Each marriage past the second has a tendency to
last shorter and shorter periods of time. There
appears to be, in failed third marriages, less trying.
The participants appear resigned to marriages which
don't work. Disillusionment encompasses the concept
of marriage.

> In my next marriage, I'll probably make the
> same dumb mistakes. I never learn anything.
> -Meg, 39 years old.

Some women, like Martha, come to accept a definition
of themselves as perpetual losers.

Three Time Losers: Further Alterations of Self

There is a clear difference between females who
are still engaged in third marriages and those who are
presently divorced from third marriages. Those females
who are still married, despite their belief that it
won't last, maintain a stronger self-concept. They
feel a sense of confidence their sisters lack. They
have it made, at least for now. Those females who are
divorced experience even greater amounts of anomie
and ambivalence after the third divorce than the
second. But not for the same reasons. In the second
divorce, many of these women rearranged their lives
during the attempts to adjust to husbands with the
end result being divorce anyway. They felt inadequate
because their adjustment attempts were unsuccessful.

The third marriage was entered into by females generally with a sense of having somewhat more control over their lives. They refused to undergo a repeat of the extreme amounts of adjustment called for in the second marriage. And so, when these third marriages end, females begin to examine their behavior, and ultimately, the costs of having control. Having control, being more autonomous, is now conceptualized as no longer being an asset. It is seen as the impetus to yet another divorce. These females attempt to begin all over again the establishment of a new social self. The feeling is that having failed at control, perhaps they should now revert back to dependence on a man.

> After three marriages I have decided that a lot of my problems is this need for independence. I should get over that. I don't want to spend all my life on a telephone pole (telephone installer). I don't need to prove anything to anyone. I need to allow myself to be dependent more on a man.
> —Sheila, after third divorce.

> If I got married again I would change some things, change some aspects about myself. I would be more subservient, less independent. I would let the man take the lead this time. I always took the lead before.
> —Lois, after third divorce.

> We never really went to church before but we go now. I've turned back to God. I think God can help me change some things about myself. I think He can make me less dominant, and less castrating.
> —Frieda, after third divorce.

For some of these females, the third divorce brings forth a completed circle. They are now back again to the starting point. There is a renewed need to belong to, to become bonded with a man. There is an attempt to buy back into the traditional role of the female. Perhaps now, this time, it will work. Nothing else has, may this. And the search goes on and on. The trying on of different social identities, varying personal philosophies and behavior patterns until hopefully one is found which has the potential of securing a lasting identity.

The Masculine Response to Divorce Crisis

For male multi-marriers, the exit out of the
second marriage and entry into the third marriage
follows a path similar to that which is traveled by
female multi-marriers. As mentioned previously, for
a few of the males, the time period following the
second divorce is one which is spent in reflection,
a period utilized for working through interactional
problems. Some deliberately avoid becoming too
involved with females, past experience has taught
that involvement usually leads to marriage. A few
others, after waiting several years, remarry for the
third time and describe their marriages as good.

> The difference between this marriage and
> the others, what makes this marriage good,
> is that we both have the same ideals, the
> same goals. Before I married women who
> were too young, only interested in money.
> This time we are both looking for the same
> damn thing. We both want a home and there
> is no hassle about it.
> -Jeff, 37 years old, whose present wife
>   is 8 years older than he.

The above statement is from a man who dated his
present wife for over two years prior to marrying her.
His first two marriages occurred after extremely
short courtships.

For those men who ended up divorced for the third
time, generally they entered into that third marriage
much like one hops on a moving train. Once on the
matrimonial road, it appears to be extremely difficult
for male multi-marriers to exist. After leaving the
second marriage, there is a tendency to become very
rapidly involved with another woman. Most of the
respondents who were presently divorced from their
third spouses had divorced the second wife, courted
and married the third, and finally divorced her all
well within an average of three years. For some,
courting, marrying and divorcing the third wife
occurred within three months. One man, presently
engaged to be married for the fifth time, describes
the process of multiple marriage extremely well.

> I got married because I wanted to get hold
> of something and be like everyone else. I
> wanted what everyone else had. The problem

139

was, getting married for me was like falling
forward. I would never regain my balance.
I would run into the next one, continue
falling and run into the next one. Sort of
like dominoes falling forward. I never had
a chance to stop and catch my breath. I
always kept right on falling.
    -Fred, 37 years old, divorced 4 times.

Many of these multi-marriers appear to be caught
up in the process of falling forward. They fall and
never give themselves time to think about marriage,
about its meaning for them or the ways in which they
go about engaging in it. For these men, the concept
of single time is an alien affair.

There is still a strong tendency to utilize
marriage as a response to role obligations. Having
grown up in an era of lesser sexual enlightenment,
marriage is often seen as the natural result of
intercourse. For some of these males, marriage is
little more than sexual involvement with a female.

The reason I get married so much is that
I'm easy. I get drunk, get a hard on, and
get married.
            -Will, divorced 5 times.

I guess most of my marriages have been based
on sex. I keep telling you that I end up
getting divorced because of greener pastures.
After I have been married for a while other
women start looking real good and I'm like
the God damn bull in the pasture, the cows
on the other side of the fence look real
good.
            -John, divorced 6 times.

The Difference Between Saying and Doing

There exists a dicotomy between the vocabulary
utilized by these men to describe the ideal of marriage and what appears to constitute their actual
marriages. The same men who responded above by
providing an understanding of the sexual nature of
their motivation for repeated marriages are also
capable of providing a vocabulary for defining marriage which any marriage therapist would readily
cherish.

140

"What is marriage, what does it mean to you?"

Being good friends, no domination and maintaining your own identity.
                    -Will, divorced five times.

I want someone to be completely honest with
me, to share with me.
                    -Mark, divorced three times.

Marriage is a bond between two people. You
have given your life to share.
                    -John, 39, divorced six times.

     Male multi-marriers appear to marry in order to
meet role obligations which operate to insure legiti-
mation of sexual intercourse. Since there is a
tendency to rapidly engage in sexual relationships
after each divorce, it is not unusual to find that
these men have also remarried again at a rather fast
pace. To be involved sexually with a woman is to
insure that marriage will also occur. However,
despite the fact that these men are inadvertently
pushed into marriage through role obligations they
are not immune to the cultural forces at play in
society today which initiate an idealism of marriage.
Thus these men have at their disposal a vocabulary to
describe marriage which in very few ways actually reflects the marriages they engage in.

Rejection of Single Time: Reinforced

Role Expectations

     Few male multi-marriers take advantage of single
time and consequently continue to fall into one
marriage after another. Like their female counterparts, male multi-marriers tend to remarry more
rapidly with each succeeding divorce. Very little
time is spent in courtship and the majority of the
courtship is tied up in interactions of a sexual
nature. There is no time for discussions of goals
and values. As with previous marriages, there is a
belief that both participants in the relationship must
share the same ideas about marriage since they share
the same bed.

     This lack of goal clarification between male
multi-marriers and their spouses is manifested all too
clearly at the time of divorce. Strong conflicts in

values, expectations, and ideals pertaining to marriage are indicated as the motivating factor in decisions to divorce.

The following men when discussing their third divorce, give evidence to the notion that little communication occurs between marriage partners prior to marriage.

> The lifestyle I thought I wanted and she wanted too didn't work. She just didn't want it. She doesn't fit in. I want to belong to the country club and she wants to fish.
>
> > -Mark, 36.

> We dated for a couple of months before we got married. It wasn't until after we were married that I found out she couldn't keep a job and that she took drugs.
>
> > -Fred, 37.

> We got married and everything changed. She got possessive and wanted me to stay at home with her. I still wanted to go out to bars and ride my motorcycle. She thought getting married meant we wouldn't be on the go all the time.
>
> > -Will, 30.

Another factor which may aid in the destruction of these marriages is a residue left over from the second marriage. Even after two marriages there is a continuing tendency on the part of these men to characterize a successful marriage as happenstance or luck. These men still, to a certain degree, buy into the myth of the marriage made in heaven.

> If I get married again it will be something that will just happen and when it happens I will just know it's right. If circumstances were right and it felt right, I would do it.
>
> > -David, 30.

Chance, luck, the right timing, the right circumstances are all viewed by these individuals as elements which go into the formation of a successful marriage. There is a belief that if one marriage does not work out, then perhaps the next one will.

Given the fact that there is a certain element of chance inserted into their definition of the requirements for a solid marriage, it is little wonder that these men do not waste time remaining in a marriage which they view as bad. A poor marriage is seen as an erroneous roll of the dice and the tendency is to divorce quickly and get back into the game. Perhaps the next roll of the dice will produce a winning play.

Given the fact that a good marriage is viewed as luck, there is little reason, in the minds of the respondents, to dwell on past history. Little introspection is experienced by these men. When marriage fails, blame is not internalized. Fault lies with the spouse or poor luck. This tendency to set aside responsibility for failed marriages is illustrated well by one of the respondents.

> I won't do anything different in my next marriage. I don't feel I have failed in marriage. On a day to day basis I have done alright. My marriages were simply situational incidents. My marriage, the way I do marriage, is all right.
> —Mark, 36.

This belief has fortified this particular respondent through three divorces.

The Emergence of a Self-fulfilling Prophecy

For Males

After a series of failed marriages, there is a tendency on the part of male multi-marriers to begin to doubt their ability to secure a stable marriage. Burned twice, many are dubious of the success of yet another marriage. Some may feel that perhaps their bad luck will never change and for those few men who took advantage of single time, there is the bitter knowledge of the sheer difficulty involved in process of working out any marital relationship. These men, like their female counterparts, often enter into third marriages fully expecting them to fail.

> I had doubts about all my marriages lasting before I married except for the fourth and I really wanted that marriage to last.
> —David, 30, divorced four times.

> I guess I have trouble staying married
> because people get on my nerves. I can't
> afford to love anyone because something
> is going to happen so you don't get close
> to people and you don't get hurt. I never
> entered any marriage except the first
> expecting it to last. But I guess it
> doesn't matter because I still get married
> . . . It's human nature to want to get
> married.
>
> —Will, divorced five times.

Working in conjunction with the emergence of this
self-fulfilling prophecy of eventual failure in
marriage is the tendency on the part of male multi-
marriers to marry younger women. The majority of
second and third wives are usually around ten years
younger than the respondents. These men appear to
purposely seek relationships with younger women.

> I like younger women. I can offer a
> younger woman some things that I can't
> offer to someone my own age.
>
> —Mark, 36.

> She was 18 and I was 32. (laughing) Note
> a bit of difference there, did you? She
> was 'hot damn' good-looking and the old
> grass was greener again. I don't think
> the age difference was a real problem.
> I could still dance all night at 32 and
> not to be bragging, but sexually I was
> still all together. I really don't know
> why all my wives are so much younger
> than I am. Maybe it's just the younger
> ones are so much better looking.
>
> —John, 39.

Male multi-marriers, tied to male sex sterotypes,
tend to conceptualize women as being the property of
the husband. Given this notion then, the respondents
have a tendency to marry women who, through sheer
youth and beauty, have the ability to reflect back to
their men enhancing attributes.

However, while these men are actively seeking
relationships with younger women who will function
positively to increase personal esteem, they are at
the same time setting up circumstances which will
eventually produce problematic areas.

> Sure, she was gorgeous and I felt proud to
> be with her. Men would look at her and I
> felt like a king because I was the one with
> her. But I always knew, even from the
> beginning that it wasn't going to work. I
> would mention baseball cards from bubble
> gum or The Platters and Twilight Time and
> she wouldn't know what I was talking about.
> My past she hadn't even been born in. For
> example, we went to see American Graffiti
> and she didn't see all the humor in it.
> Hell, that was my childhood!
>
> —John, 39.

For others the differences in age related to more
concrete matters which directly affected the marital
relationship.

> She is concerned that I might get tired of
> the whole situation and leave, and she is
> probably right. I knew when I first married
> her that there would come a day when she
> would want to have a child. I have no plans
> for any more children and when that day does
> arrive, we will split.
>
> —Charles, 41, father of three children
> from previous marriages.

Men marry younger women in order to enhance their
social identities, while intuitively understanding
that doing so will aid in the destruction of that
marriage. The notion of a self-fulfilling prophecy
is reinforced.

A Masculine Difference in Serial Marriages

There is one final element in the masculine
road to multiple marriage which sets this course off
as opposed to the route taken by females. As earlier
discussed, females perceive time as an enemy for the
most part. The years bring a component of aging
which they fear and hate. A certain portion of this
anxiety over age relates to their ability to successfully bear and raise children. Those who have not
completed a family yet feel an urge to hurry and find
a mate before it is too late. This sense of urgency
is not experienced by male multi-marriers. There is
little concern over fatherhood. When these men speak
of settling down and building a home, for the most
part, children are not considered to be a part of the

145

scenario. Off-spring compose only a very small portion
of the male multi-marrier's social world.

When a marriage ends in divorce, any ties which
may bind the two spouses together are irrevocably
broken. There is no looking back. Any children
which may have been produced by the marriage are seen
as belonging to the wife. Children are womens' work.
With rare exception, children are no longer seen by
their fathers and few men even contribute child
support. There is little emotional bonding with
children.

> Yeah, I do have a child. I have a son.
> He's 10 or 11 now, I guess. No, he may
> even be 12. I would have to stop and
> think about that.
>> -Will, age 30, father of one
>> by his first marriage.

> Let me see. I guess my son is 10 now. I
> haven't seen him since he was a baby. I
> don't send any money to him, or any child
> support. I paid her a sum of money at the
> time of divorce for him. I suppose maybe
> someday I will look him up when he is an
> adult and get to know him then.
>> -Tom, 39, father of one child
>> by his first marriage.

> I see my youngest daughter some times. I
> run into her at the cafe sometimes. Of
> course, she calls me Jim and thinks of
> me as Jim. I don't know if she knows I'm
> her father or not.
>> -John, 39, father of three daughters.

> "Do you want her to know you as her father?"

> Oh, I guess not. Doesn't really matter.
> When her mother and I divorced she (the
> ex-wife) never hassled me about child
> support so I figured the girl was really
> her's to do what she wanted to with.

Ties are maintained with children, however nominal,
only if a set sum of child support is paid periodically. If men do not pay child support, then the off-
spring are seen as belonging to the wife totally. No
contact is maintained with ex-wives or children. Just

as wives are seen as enhancing property to many of
these men, children also are conceptualized as
property, and after the divorce the children become
the total property of the wife.

Perhaps the last statement seems harsh. This
researcher really does not know how to soften it
without loosing the context of meaning applied by
men as they perceive their children. Perhaps given
the rugged, authoritarian fathers these men were
exposed to as children, it may well be simply a
re-enactment of their own relationships with their
fathers. One also needs to bear in mind that multi-
marriers tend to marry others like them, often
choosing females who have been divorced at least once.
Both males and females who marry frequently have a
tendency to insist on complete cessation of all interactions at the time of divorce. It may be that this
lack of communication between fathers and sons is a
situation created by ex-wives.

Despite what appears to be for some of the female
respondents a deep concentration on finding a mate
and having children before it is too late, there is
an amazingly small number of children. Ten female
respondents accounted for only 11 children, with one
respondent being the mother of four of these children.
The eight male respondents contributed 11 children,
with one male being the father of three daughters.
This is an interesting contradiction. Females who
advocate children have overall less children than
males who appear to be at most only nominally interested in fatherhood. Over all, multiple marriers
appear to have less children on the average than those
individuals who marry only once. Of course, it does
take time to produce children, and for many of these
people, marriages simply do not last long enough to
produce off-spring.

The Many Times Married

Three of the respondents interviewed were
individuals who were presently married or divorced
from their fifth marriage. There is one thread that
ties the experience of these people together. Each
succeeding marriage was undertaken after a short
courtship, shorter than the one preceding it, and the
marriage lasted less time than the one it followed.
For these three individuals, marriage can best be
described as a merry-go-round. They are much like

children at a circus. They climb on the merry-go-round and never want to get off. They continue going round and round, occasionally changing horses, but never staying with one for very long. These are people who are dismayed at their own history. They are embarrassed and saddened by their inability to sustain a marital relationship. They want a successful marriage but they simply do not know how to go about obtaining it. Some are bitter and most are afraid. They are, in a very real sense, their own worst enemy.

I want to have a lasting marriage but I always end up choosing the wrong woman. I know they are wrong when I choose them but I do it anyway.

"If you realize they are wrong, why do you think you marry anyway?"

If I choose the right one, they would expect you to get close and I can't do that. I can't let anyone get close.
-John, 39 years old, divorced six times.

I've faced the fact that I will never be able to do it, make a good marriage. I'm one of those people who were never meant to be happy. I guess I will always be alone. I'll try to marry again, I know that, but I'll just screw up again.
-Meg, 39, divorced five times.

Summary

Sequential marriers are individuals who, in a very real sense, feel little control over their own destiny. Much of life is conceptualized as luck or chance. They are individuals who have seen the satisfaction others are able to derive from marriage and want very badly to have this for their own. Unfortunately, they have no idea how to go about obtaining it.

A few, after the second divorce, are able to take advantage of single time and analyze past mistakes. These are the individuals who have come to some understanding that perhaps marriage is an active process, an experiment in living which requires the two participating parties to both have input in the relationship.

148

For the rest, those who go on to have three, four, and even five marriages, there is no time for reflection. The past is put behind them as quickly as possible and is never looked at again. They continue falling, like dominoes, from one marriage right into another, inwardly hoping that someone special will catch them as they fall and break the cycle of multiple marriages.

CHAPTER VII

CONCLUSION

This research effort constitutes an exploratory investigation into the process of multiple marriage. The limiting nature of an exploratory study necessitates the absence of grand theorizing, predictive correlates, and definitive postulates. This study meets those requirements. The primary goal of this research effort was to take a relatively unknown social phenomenon, multiple marriage, and create for the reader a more intimate understanding of it. Its intent, in Lofland's (1971) words, was simply to make that which was "known about" just a little bit more "known". This study was designed to come to some understanding of the social world of a special category of persons, the multi-marriers, by presenting their interpretation of their world. This researcher believes this work has achieved its goals.

However, inasmuch as every research effort, no matter how meager its origins, is expected to add to a body of existing knowledge by drawing certain conclusions from its findings, this expectation will also be met to a certain degree. The process of multiple marriage is exceedingly complex. This inherent complexity makes fundamental insight difficult, however, as an exploratory study some tenuous observations can be made. The intent and purpose of publication of these observations is for utilization as possible routes for future, more extensive investigations, certainly not as an end in itself, but rather a beginning.

The complexity of multiple marriage is due to its many encompassing elements, some more critical than others, and all interplaying to a certain extent with each other simultaneously. At times, it appears a futile effort to assess the component parts of multiple marriage and hold any one element up for audience viewing and shout victoriously, "I have it! This is multiple marriage!", for at the very moment you have isolated any one critical factor, the process of multiple marriage, being dynamic, has already moved ahead and left remaining in your hands little more than history.

The above statement is not meant to discount the importance of history, for it is history in a very real

150

sense which gives substance to our lives. However, in terms of analyzing multiple marriage, history is simply, and consequently ultimately, an element in time past. It is an experience which can be used for building on the present and the future but cannot be utilized for representing the whole. For this reason, we have presented the biographies of multi-marriers in a historical sense in order to see a progression from one phase into another, the overlapping of one symbolic episode with the next. It was thought that this particular type of presentation would allow for the visual emergence of altered meanings and definitions as they occur within the life course of the multi-marrier.

Within the body of data, whenever one particular point seemed critical, it was analyzed and discussed at that time rather than elaborated on at the conclusion of the work. It seemed more appropriate to understand the impact of a critical element in the process of multiple marriage at the very time of its influence rather than set it aside for later study. The end result of this type of analysis is a rather micro view of the emerging processes of multiple marriage as one phase ends and another begins. Of course, this was the intent of the study. However, in terms of placing closure on this research effort, it is now time to step back and view this phenomenon more wholistically, to move beyond the relational scope of one phase building on another, and to try to place the entire process into some type of coherent order.

The Search for Social Order

The Meaning of Marriage

Fontana (1977) has noted that

various sociological theories have explored
the extent to which man imbeds the meaning
of his life in various structures in society,
and while they by no means agree on the
nature of this structuring, there exists a
general consensus that man crowds his life
with preestablished normative meanings which
allow him to proceed relatively undisturbed
through his existence (p. 16).

Throughout the historical biographies of multiple marriers, there appears to be one constant theme, an imbedded meaning, which guides and directs the actions of these persons as they engaged in the process of serial marriage. This generic theme will be called the search for social order.

Played out numerous times through many marriages, by the creation and dissolution of various relationships, by the isolation of parent from child, through the narcotic effect of drugs and alcohol, expressed through episodes of family violence and frequent identity reorganizations, is the continual quest for some sense of social order around which to organize social life. Multiple marriers, by their own admission, are individuals who have experienced few, if any, substantial periods of social order and are, by deficit, compelled to initiate situations in which hopes for a sense of social order can be achieved. Several respondents in this study identified themselves and their counter-parts as searchers. They conceptualize themselves as seekers of stability through marriage. Marriage is seen as social order.

The immediate question which arises, of course, is why marriage should be viewed as social order. Why is so much meaning, in terms of the ability to organize and stabilize social life, imbedded in marriage? This, given the instability of childhood exposures to marriage, is an interesting, although problematic question. A partial response to the question lies, theoretically, not in alignment with role-modeling and other theories which concentrate on childhood learning experiences, but rather in opposition to those particular paradigms. Given the fact that most of the respondents were not exposed to what they define as particularly good marriages, and certainly, by history, the parental marriages appeared to these persons to be without longevity or substance, it would seem that these individuals would internalize messages which would indicate to them that marriages are relationships which do not last. To this extent, a surface observation of the numerous marriages of the respondents appear to support notions of role-modeling or what Muller and Pope (1977) have referred to as the intergenerational transmission of divorce. However, closer observation of the meanings attached to various marriages alter the traditional perspective associated with role-modeling.

Multi-marriers may, in effect, act as if they hold little faith in the longevity of the marriage relationship, by dissolving marital relationships, but when discussing the meaning of marriage with these individuals, it is shown quite clearly that these are persons who adamantly invest marriage with the notion of longevity. Marriage is entered into with the belief that it will be a lifetime commitment. In short, there is a discrepancy between what multi-marriers profess to believe, and by rights according to childhood marriages should not believe, and the actual results of a strong belief system.

Multi-marriers, by history, should not view marriage as social order. As children, they were not exposed to the act of marriage as social order, yet over and over they express the notion that marriage is very much the foundation of social order for them. One possible explanation for this discrepancy and polarization between childhood socialization and internalized adult belief systems deals directly with the diminishing influence of the family as the primary agent of socialization. Multi-marriers, as children, may have been raised in physical isolation from others due to frequent moves, and consequently have been left with few ties to people or places, but it should be clear that they were not raised in social isolation. The extent to which they have formed the meaning of marriage as a long-term relationship in opposition to what they were exposed to as children, demonstrates the input of others beyond the immediate family.

Blumer (1969) has suggested that the meaning of a thing grows out of the ways in which others act toward the person with regard to the thing. The meaning of marriage, then, as social order, evolved from a type of social interaction and communication with unknown others outside the immediate family. From Reiseman's (1950) perspective, with regard to marriage, multiple marriers are very much a prototype of the otherdirected individual, at least to the extent that they look to the greater society at large for direction in understanding the meaning of marriage as social order. The majority of these individuals were raised within a religious environment which stressed the biblical interpretation of marriage as a lifetime commitment. Perhaps media also influenced their interpretation of marriage. This is suggested by one woman's mournful lament of the failure of marriage to be like Hart to Hart.

The scope of this study was not designed to
measure the extent of the influence of others on the
formation of the meaning of marriage, so it is
impossible to cite the various variables which may
have joined together to aid in defining marriage
for these individuals. It is enough at this point
to note that multi-marriers were, as children,
despite situations which suggest otherwise,
very open to the input of others beyond the scope
of the immediate family. To this extent, social
learning theories which concentrate on a mineless
repetition of social acts are erroneous, at least
in terms of explaining the process of multiple marriage
for the respondents.

The Residue of Childhood Experiences

Since the meanings applied to marriage
by the respondents are not necessarily dependent on
childhood experiences, then what is left from the
childhood biographies of these persons? In observing
the life course of multi-marriers, there appears
to be one crucial element which still has effect on
adult experiences. This is the notion that social
interaction is not dependent on negotiation. As
children, serial marriers were not in a position to
witness the importance of negotiation in the sustaining of social relationships. The young multi-
marrier was reared by an authoritative father, a
powerful individual who made judgements arbitrarily
and fully expected decisions to be enacted immediately
without discussion. Through interaction with this
very significant other, multi-marriers rapidly
internalized the notion that social relationships
are not dependent on negotiation. As children,
they observed the effects of the decision making
and implementing power of others on their own lives
and perhaps began to think that all of social life
operated on the same premise.

The idea that social interaction is not dependent
on negotiation is seen in the obvious lack of negotiation displayed in the many marriages perpetrated
by these individuals. As mentioned in previous
chapters, multi-marriers are persons who do not place
much stock in the power of talk. Discussions of poor
marital relationships are not entered into with
spouses. Decisions to enter into and exit from a

marriage are expressed through activity, they are not communicated to others through discussion. Social interaction, and therefore, social relationships, are viewed as consisting largely of expressed behavior, with vocalization not being seen as activity. The acting out of a decision is seen to be the foundation of communication. Talk is not viewed as communication. This culminates in the tendency on the part of the respondents to conceptualize social relationships not as joint activity, but rather focuses attention on the drama of the situation of marriage, with the casting of self as a singular actor and the spouse as a passive viewing audience.

To the extent that any childhood messages are learned from family life and internalized, it is the powerless of negotiation in social relationships which proves crucial to the adult experience. As children, with few having long term connections with people or places, thus being denied the opportunity to see the necessity of negotiation in sustaining social interaction, these individuals are persons who possess an interactional handicap. They desperately want the strength of stability in marriage yet lack the capacity for achieving it, for they fail to see the significance of communication as a basis for sustained interaction. These are people who are not tied to the notion of symbolic communication through language.

The effects of not being tied to communication as a means to sustain social relationships are seen in resulting divorces. Jourard (1975), in discussing his notion of marriage as a lifetime choice suggests that,

> marriage at its best, according to the image that is making the most sense to me, is a relationship within which change is generated by the very way of relating-dialogue, so that growth as well as identity and a sense of rootedness are engendered (p. 199).

Multi-marriers,immersed in an interactional pattern which denies communication, or dialogue, as a result experience very little growth or rootedness. Their sense of social order is rooted not in the marital relationship, so to speak, but rather in their image of what constitutes marriage. In essence, it is a denial of the social nature of marriage and a concentration on the fixed image of marriage. This idea of a fixed image of marriage will be discussed at length later on. For the present, an understanding of the non-social nature of marriage for the respondents is at issue, particularly as it is implied through their determined sense of the non-importance of dialogue.

Due to the lack of negotiation in interaction, multi-marriers can be seen as behaviorally actors and reactors, with symbolic communication through dialogue having little effect on social relationships. A question arises at this point. Why should there be a symbolic communication to these persons that the meaning of marriage is based on a lifetime commitment while the symbolic nature of communication through dialogue is interrupted? Unfortunately, there is no set answer. Perhaps, due to the impact of family violence which occurred when negotiation with significant others was attempted as children, the lesson of the noneffectiveness of negotiation in social relationships was rather physically internalized while the notion of the symbolic meaning of marriage was not quite so dramatically displayed.

As Journard (1975) suggested, a lack of rootedness is the result of a lack of communication. Multi-marriers are individuals who grew up with few roots. As children, they were not exposed to long-term interactions which were dependent on bargaining skills and often they interacted with significant others who denied negotiation by power positions. In short, their exposure to the social world of relationships simply did not stress the notion of joint constructions of reality. To borrow a term from Goffman (1969), multi-marriers are not good team members. The extent to which the non-negotiable aspect of marriage carries over into social avenues of human life and the exact process by which this interactional barrier emerges cannot be answered by the limited nature of an exploratory study. At this time and point, it is enough to suggest, in accordance with Journard's (1975) perspective, that non-dialogic ways of being married are either exercised in a chronic struggle for power and control or they are habors to escape those aspects of life that would engender growth.

The Differential Search for Social Order

It has been suggested that for multi-marriers marriage is seen as a search for social order. However, throughout the course of data presentation, the differential experience of males and females with regard to marriage has been emphasized. While it is true that men and women perceive and experience their social worlds differently, it is also true that these two sexes are members of the same species, and as such, some commonality in perception must guide both sexes in the social arena. It has been suggested that the search for social order through marriage, defined differentially by males and females, is the unifying thread for men and women. In essence, it is not the meaning of marriage as social order which is at question due to sex differences, but rather the definitional processes involved whereby each sex comes to experience self in relationship to social order which generates a unique perception for men and women.

In earlier chapters, it has been suggested that the essential difference in men and women with regard to definitions of self in marriage is simplistically the difference between "doing" and "being". The notion of "doing", for males, connotates a turning to achievements in the outer and 'real' world, thus creating a situation in which the males come to place value on himself in terms of objective criteria. The male is "pressured by his own impulses and by society's demands to give up depending predominately on the response of others for feelings of self-esteem" (Bardwick and Douvan, 1977, p. 256). He is guided away from the social nature of interpersonal relationships as a basis for validation. The young man perceives his search for social order to revolve around a strict adherence to role obligations. To succeed in adequately responding to role requirements is seen as effectively securing goals, achieving manhood.

The female multi-marrier, raised within an early environment which sensitized her to the importance of social relationships, to the point that she perceives self only in relational terms with others, grows acutely aware of her dependency on an interactional "other". Without a husband, the all important "other", her sense of social order is disarrayed and the need to continually seek an interactional "other" is played out over and over again through remarriage.

Berger and Kellener (1974) have suggested that marriage can be considered in our society as a dramatic act in which two strangers come together and redefine themselves. Marriage, in this sense, for young males can be seen as a definitional process whereby they come to see themselves as accepting responsibility and fulfilling role obligations. Marriage, as a culturally accepted admission of adulthood, is the embodiment of social order and the cultural directive for manhood. One achieves marriage, much as one achieves any other goal in life, and the actual marriage act itself is sufficient validation of self. Male multi-marriers, through the act of marriage, can then define themselves as having achieved social order. An interpersonal relationship with a spouse is not a necessary part of the definition of social order.

However, the female multi-marrier, geared to the social nature of relationships, and being dependent on others for definition of self, spends the majority of her adulthood attempting to secure a completed social identity through a marital relationship which is essentially secure and safe. The notion of marriage as an on-going daily enactment represents to her the process whereby she is assured of an interactional "other", a completed social identity, and thus enables her to define self in relationship to marriage. Marriage, as the assurance of "other", is, for the female, social order.

For both men and women, marriage represents a sense of social order. Each sex attempts to secure for themselves a sense of social order differentially, by defining themselves in relationship to marriage quite uniquely, however, it is still the meaning of marriage as social order which is the underlying factor which guides conduct for both sexes. Marriage, either as exemplification of role obligations or as the necessary counter-part of a whole social identity, is the generic process whereby multi-marriers make sense out of their social world.

Marriage as a Fixed Image

In following the biographies of multiple marriers throughout the course of several marriages, it was noted that most multi-marriers share a common interactional barrier, the inability to participate in negotiation. This deficit in interactional skills created, for many, problematic areas in the marital relationship which ultimately led to divorce. For a few respondents, the ability to participate in new forms of social interaction, thus enabling new ways of defining self in relationship to marriage, developed as a result of "single time". For these individuals, social change occurred. However, for the majority, the incorporation of new interactional skills was negated and these persons continued to play out marriage dramas which were destined for failure.

Given the fact that the search for social order through marriage is an imperative in the lives of multiple marriers, why is this particular quest so problematic for them? It is true that there are individuals who, for a variety of reasons, lack the interpersonal skills necessary for sustaining long-term interaction, however, the inability to secure a stable marriage is strongly influenced by one insurmountable obstacle which prevents multi-marriers from gaining the skills necessary for performing a successful marriage. Multi-marriers have a tendency to perceive all elements in their social world which relate directly to marriage as absolutes. A marriage which is evaluated as good is maintained and a marriage which is judged as bad is dissolved. As in social relationships, there is no negotiation of the basic format which composes their notion of marriage.

For the multi-marrier, the notion of marriage is surrounded by what appears to be a perpetual belief in an ideal-type. The fixed image nature of marriage is very much like the fixed image some attach to a strong religious ideology, that being the belief in an everlasting happiness with God. For the multi-marrier, marriage, in effect, transposes the position of God and marriage then indicates a state of perpetual happiness. Just as some persons in this society turn to God to organize and direct their social existence, so do multi-marriers place the same expectations for social order as being derived from marriage. And, just as God is perfect, so too must be the evaluation placed on any one marriage.

So strong is this belief in marriage as an ideal-type, that marriage, any marriage, is compared to its fixed image nature, and any relationship which fails to meet the total requirements set out by this ideal-type, is judged inadequate. Marriage, or rather the concept of marriage as an ideal-type, is seen as an absolute. Individual marriages are compared and if found lacking in any of the component parts of the fixed image, are dissolved by divorce. This notion of an ideal-type for marriage is characterized by the refusal on the part of the respondents to label marriage, in and of itself, as evil or the instigator in any one divorce. Time and again, blame for the dissolution of marriage is placed on the inability of the multi-marrier to adequately choose an appropriate partner.

Coexisting with, and consequently reinforcing the fixed image of marriage, is what Jourard (1975, p. 199) has referred to as "the myth of the right partner". The myth of the right partner is expressed by multi-marriers in their descriptions of the perfect spouse as being "Mr. Right". When marriages dissolve, the ideal-type nature of marriage is maintained by assessing the degeneration to have stemmed from faulty mate selection processes. The integrity of marriage is sustained by conceptualizing divorce to be the result of not having secured the right partner.

A mystical quality, stemming from the belief in an ideal-type marriage, is inserted into the decision making process of mate selection. Luck, or chance, or fate is seen as the major ingredient necessary for appropriate spouse selection. Thus, just as an ideal marriage is viewed as the ultimate goal in male-female relationships, so too is a selection process which appropriately chooses the perfect mate for the perfect marriage. Negotiation of the marital relationship is then effectively denied as a necessary part of marriage, for if the right partner had been chosen, then negotiation would not be necessary. Should any type of negotiation be called for, or demanded by the spouse, the circular nature of the image of marriage comes into play and divorce is the response. Obviously, if the partner chosen for marriage is wrong, then that particular marriage is not an ideal-type marriage and must be dissolved.

The Creation of the Fixed Image of Marriage

At this point, one is drawn to examine the intensity of this notion of ideal-types. Why is it that multi-marriers are individuals who are guided by such

a strong belief system which incorporates the notion
of the ideal-type marriage played out with the perfect
partner, to the extent that compromise is denied and
any relationship which is in need of negotiation is
discounted and discarded? Again, as with other questions brought to light by this study, no definitive
answer emerges but rather, a suggestive route is
taken.

In a very real sense, multiple marriers are
individuals who are trapped between two worlds, the
old and the new, the traditional and the modern, with
the end result of this ambiguous incarceration being
the production of marginal men and women. Having been
raised in an environment which stressed more traditional lifestyles, at least in terms of adherence to sex
roles, there are persons who have been forced to spend
the majority of their lives in a social world for which
they are poorly equipped, a world of rapidly changing
values, morals, meanings, and definitions.

The multi-marriers involved in this study generally come from lower class families, family types
which have been noted for their more traditional lifestyles, and perhaps the foundation for the early beginnings of the process of multiple marriage lies
within that class reference. However, for the majority
of the respondents, while having origins in an environment of poverty, by adulthood had somehow managed to
elevate their social class standing by their own sheer
efforts. It may be at this point that the intertwining
of two social class ideologies becomes confusing and
aids in the creation of a lifestyle of serial marriage.

Lederer and Jackson (1968) state:

The institution of marriage has failed to
adapt itself sufficiently to current requirements. The constant battle of the
sexes and the family turmoil raging today
are evidence of the haphazard efforts of
individuals to reconcile their traditional
role images with current realities. With
little help from any social quarter, men
and women are fighting a lonely battle to
find their place in the sun. Plagued by
guilt and uncertainty, they struggle to
discover their 'identity' yet are unable
to accept themselves if they do catch a
glimpse of their genuine needs, desires,

and goals. For what they glimpse is not what
they have been conditioned to believe is
'good' or 'right' according to age-old
systems of belief, developed on the basis of
requirements which died at the time of the
Industrial Revolution (p. 35).

As Udry (1966) has pointed out, most Americans do not
really know what happens after marriage although we
certainly have expectations based on various romantic
dreams. In terms of marriage, we have a tendency to
focus on a fantasy image of marriage which implies that
the marital arrangement is an assurance of continual
security in a very insecure world. Of course, multi-
marriers are more strongly tied to fantasy images than
most. For them, coming from a socialization process
which tends to instill the notion of role adherence
more stringently than other environments, it is possible to understand why these are also individuals who
would be closely tied to an ideal component of cultural
messages. Roles, in terms of conceptualizations of
maleness and femaleness, structure their social world
and blend together in a tendency to sustain a notion
of an ideal-type. Lederer and Jackson (1968) have
further advised that "if modern marriage is to be
successful, not only the assignment of roles, but
other traditional attitudes and practices as well must
be revised" (p. 18). For the multi-marrier, less
rigidity in the conceptualization of the fixed image
nature of marriage and the myth of the perfect partner
is called for.

The Problematic Nature of Multiple

Marriage for Society

Individuals who participate in serial marriage
have at various times been labeled with such psychological terms as neurotic or psychotic. Multiple
marriers are not necessarily individuals with psychological deficits. The deficiency, if one chooses to
label incomplete interactional skills as a deficiency,
falls squarely within the realm of the social world,
not the psychological. From a sociological perspective,
there is no real pathology in serial marriage.

The problem for society, in dealing with this
category of person, is the extent to which they focus

on marriage as the ultimate validating experience.
Other members of our society choose to apply ideal-
type constructions to different forms of social
organization without a similar dedication being quite
so problematic. The religious leader is allowed to
profess a faith in a perfect God, the educator is
encouraged to argue for an adequate educational system
and the politician is given leniency in lobbying for
a particular bill without suffering a similar social
disorganization as that which plagues multi-marriers.

The tendency on the part of some to label the
process of multiple marriage as strange or pathological
stems from two sources. Social life is predicated on
the notion of interaction. Implied in the definition
of interaction is a certain amount of negotiation.
The sustaining of a particular reality is dependent on
the joint activities of the individuals involved in
the construction of that particular reality. Multi-
marriers are, as pointed out earlier, not very skilled
at joint activities, at least as this concept applies
to marriage realities. And, yet, despite an obvious
lack of skill, multi-marriers are individuals who
insist on continuing to try.

Our society is very oriented towards team activities. A large part of our recreational time is spent
in observing or taking part in team activities. Multi-
marriers are persons who have shown themselves to be
poor team players. They simply strike out alot and
rather than try their skill at another game where they
might prove more proficient, they demand repeated
times at bat. In a sense, multi-marriers are problematic for society for this very reason. They are an
embarrassment. We, as a society, do value marriage,
however, we do not value those who attempt marriage
frequently yet continue to fail. Multi-marriers are
losers and all losers are problematic for a society
which heralds winners.

The Future of Multiple Marriage

Normative Support of Serial Marriages

In a society which is experiencing high divorce
rates, and concurrently a high incidence of multiple
marriage, one of the major questions that is raised is

whether serial monogamy can be considered representative of an emerging marital form. From a statistical
perspective, we are aware that the rise in the incidence of multiple marriage in the past three decades
is high, however, it has not exceeded the heights to
be expected given the rise in divorce in general. An
analysis of the future of serial marriage must then
fall within the realm of supposition and extrapolation
rather than be firmly rooted in demographic findings.
In essence, what is called for is an assessment of
the various social and emotional forces at play which
join together to aid in the creation of new family
forms, which of course, are only belatedly measured by
demographic instruments after these new alternatives
have emerged and become a part of on-going society.

In terms of predicting the growth of multiple
marriage as a viable marital form, it is initially
necessary to test the waters, so to speak, by ascer-
taining whether or not any spokespersons have emerged
to provide a rationale and justification for engaging
in such a behavior pattern. Often it is the existence
of such forerunners who, in their advocacy of a particular lifestyle, set the stage for a change in cultural
norms which prohibit such behavior. Advocates of new
and freer forms of marriage relationships have a long,
if somewhat inglorious, history.

The movement to accept divorce as a response to
growing marital hostility began in the late 1800s, when
controversy was touched off by a growth in the divorce
rate. In 1880, there was one divorce for every 21
marriages; in 1900, there was one divorce for every 12
marriages; in 1909, the ratio had increased to one in
10, and by 1916, it stood at one in nine (O'Neill, 1978,
p. 141). Naturally this dramatic increase in the
divorce rate stimulated public alarm and created two
opposing factions, equally divided on the issue of mo-
rality in divorce. Early Feminists, such as Elizabeth
Cady Stanton, led a political fight to reform the
severity of divorce laws and was supported in 1904 by
historian and sociologist, George E. Howard. He argued
for the decline in the old patriarchal family and a
"new kind of marriage marked by higher spiritual
standards and greater freedom" (O'Neill, 1978, p. 146).
These early pro-divorce activists encouraged an environment which equated divorce with human freedom.

Since that time of emerging conflict, many social
philosophers and writers have argued for new family

164

forms centering primarily around the concept of trial marriage. In 1927, Judge Ben B. Lindsey proposed trial marriage in his term, "Companionate Marriage" and was supported by Bertrand Russell who extended the opinion that it was ridiculous for a couple to marry for the purpose of raising a family when they had not first had sexual experience. Margaret Mead revived this notion of trial marriage in 1966 by her proposal of a two-step marriage, and was followed by Virginia Satir in 1967 when she proposed a five-year renewal contract for marriage and was noted to have suggested that to expect people to be infallible in the selection of a life partner is to ask them to be wiser than possible. Toffler (1972, p. 251) has observed that "As a conventional marriage proves itself less and less capable of deliving on its promise of life long happiness . . . we can anticipate public acceptance of temporary marriages." Defining marriage as an out-dated institution, psychologist James Hemming predicts that the word marriage itself may become obsolete (replaced by the designation pairbound) and that individuals will marry only after having lived together for a set amount of time (Schwartz, 1968, p. 213).

In short, many advocates historically have been active in creating a social milleu which supports an ideology that places blame on an out-dated institution and in effect, allows individuals a justification for seeking new forms of marriage relationships. Given the current divorce rates presently being experienced in the United States, it is more than conceivable that the present cohort of school age children will mature into a generation of adults who accept divorce as a way of life. As Glick and Norton (1977) explain this tendency to more openly accept divorce;

> An increasingly common life course event for children today is living in a family where only one parent is present. It has been estimated that nearly one-half of all children born today will spend a meaningful portion of their lives as children in a single-parent situation before they reach the age of 18 years (Population Bulletin, #5, Vol 312, 1977).

While it is true that divorce still fosters some episodes of stigma in society today, it is well within the realm of possibility, given the environment in which our young are presently being reared, and in association with spokespersons who advocate new family forms, that serial marriage has the potential of becoming an accepted lifestyle. In short, there is evidence to indicate a tentative but growing normative culture which supports the ideology of multiple marriages. As Yankelovich (1981) has pointed out, when an NBC Associated Press poll in 1978 asked Americans whether they thought "most couples getting married today expect to remain married for the rest of their lives", a 60 percent majority said no.

Variables Affecting Multiple Major Marriage

The study of divorce has reached such a level of sophistication that we are able to postulate certain variables as having direct influence on the likelihood of a given set of persons to divorce. These same variables which increase or decrease chances to divorce, concurrently also affect the likelihood of individuals to engage in multiple marriages. Examining these attributes may shed light on the possible future of multiple marriage in this society.

The Effects of Age on Serial Marriage

The first characteristic to be examined is the factor of age as it influences divorce. It has been well documented by many social researchers that the likelihood of marital instability increases as the ages of the spouses decrease (Glick and Norton, 1971; Spanier and Glick, 1981). In the past century, the United States has experienced a decrease in the median age at first marriage for both sexes. In 1890, the median age at first marriage for males was 26.1 and 22 years for females (Current Population Reports, #365, 1981). Today, the median age is 24.6 and 22.1 respectively for both sexes. It is generally assumed that a postponment in the age of marriage is associated with advanced education and establishment of a career, both factors strongly influencing the economic status of a couple, a point which will be discussed later.

While the median age at first marriage has risen from a low of 22.5 and 20.1 in 1956, it still has not matched the rates noted in 1890. Due to the epidemic incidence of teenage pregnancy and increasing tendency

on the part of parents to support married college
children, there may be a chance to see the median age
stabilize or drop slightly, if all factors remain
equal. However, marital instability has also been
associated with lower levels of education (Spanier and
Glick, 1981). Given the present economic situation
this nation is experiencing in association with the
drying up of college funding, more young people may be
forced into an early labor market entry rather than
forego jobs for advanced education. Should this prove
to be the case, then marriage at an early age is more
likely as young people become established in the job
market sooner, perhaps resulting in more divorce as
younger, less educated couples experience marital
distress.

     In terms of applying this factor to multiple
marriage, it is evident from the sample of respondents
utilized in this research, that potential multiple
marriers begin a career of marriage earlier than the
median age experienced nationwide. The respondents
demonstrated mean ages at first marriage of 20 years
and 18 years, respectively. Inasmuch as the likelihood of remarriage, particularly for women, is greatly
increased if a first divorce occurs before the age of
thirty (Glick and Norton, 1977; Glick, 1980), then it
is logical to expect that those individuals who participate in marriage at earlier ages are more likely to
have greater opportunities at remarriage after the
initial divorce.

     In short, multiple marriers show a tendency to
marry earlier and divorce at younger ages than those
who marry and divorce only once. Should the median
age for young people at first marriage drop, then there
is an increased likelihood that we will observe greater
rates of multiple marriage. In essence, the present
political atmosphere which is advocating less educational funding and financial support in other ways may
inadvertently create an environment which allows more
youthful marriage to occur, and concurrently, increases
the likelihood of multiple marriage. This notion of
divorce being related to educational levels is best
expressed in terms of college graduates having the most
stable marriages, 85 percent of which are still engaged
in first marriages (Glick, 1975; Glick and Norton,
1977). Should we experience a decrease in the number
of college graduates in this society, we may experience
an increase in the number of divorces.

Socioeconomic Status and Serial Marriage

Another economic factor to be considered when predicting the rise of serial marriage in this society is the relationship between socioeconomic status and divorce. Divorce rates have generally been lower among individuals in the upper socioeconomic groups. Drawing from economic characteristics of the respondent sample, multiple marriage, is seen to be associated with lower socioeconomic status. To put it bluntly, the less the money, the more the divorce. Glick (1975) has suggested that these two factors are related to what he refers to as the "coping power" found among the more financially advantaged. He suggests that the development of superior coping powers may result in those who are more achievement-oriented, have more success in terms of careers and more expertise in meeting a wider variety of problems associated with advancing careers, as opposed to wage related jobs. Also implied, but not stated, in this notion of greater coping skills is the ability to financially provide greater outlets in terms of recreation and counseling for a faltering marriage as needed.

Komarovsky (1962), Rubin (1976), Farber (1964), and many others have studied the relationship between marriage satisfaction and levels of income in depth. All point to higher levels of income as having strong influence in decisions to divorce or not divorce. As Rubin (1976) suggests, it is the lack of money to pursue alternative satisfaction in life which make the disappointments in marriage so acute. When all hopes and dreams are centered on one tenuous relationship, the marriage, and validation of one's life experiences is lacking in all other areas, it may well be at that point in time that marriage becomes, as Toffler (1970) has observed, less and less capable of deliving on its promise. In terms of simple exchange theory, when a marriage is surrounded by poverty, the rewards outside the marriage may frequently surpass a lifetime of bills.

The pressures which are placed on marriage in a situation defined by too little money are enormous. Generally, lacking in education, therefore being denied access to work which is considered meaningful and fulfilling, lower income spouses spend "at least one-half of the waking hours each day doing work that is dull, routine, deadening-in a word, alienating, and

alienated labor" (Rubin, 1976, p. 160). It is expected
that substitute gratification may be found in the
private sector of life, the family, marriage, and the
home. However, a home life which consists primarily of
struggles to feed and clothe and house family members
has little potential to respond as an alternative
gratification for meaningless work. And for lower
class men, directed from early childhood to find
validation outside the home, a harsh economic situation
can almost guarantee marital dissatisfaction. Marriage,
as it is practiced today, does not have the capacity
to mediate all of life's problems encountered outside
the family.

The current economic situation defined by higher
rates of unemployment and rising inflation may well
contribute to an increase in divorce, and consequently
multiple marriage, in yet another way. By forcing more
and more women into the labor force in an effort to
stablize a family's income, the precarious economic
system is creating a means for women to secure a
validation of self which is not dependent on the role
of mother and wife. By earning money and helping in
the economic support of her family, women have inadvertently created an alteration in terms of the
traditional power arrangement of the American family.
By acknowledging an increase in her resources, the
working wife may demand more input in the daily
functioning of family life, and if this demand is not
met by her spouse, she will have the financial capacity
to leave the family home and create a home for herself
and her children which is not dependent on marriage.
As Nye (1979) has postulated,

> Among professional and executive women, the
> proportion of divorces in which the wife
> files for divorce is greater among those
> who earn more than their husbands than among
> those who earn less than their husbands (p. 27).

The ideology of the women's movement strongly
stresses a validation of self for women which is not
totally dependent on the role of wife and mother. As
more and more women are pushed outside the home into
the labor market, there is increasing normative support
for her to seek gratifications from work as well as
family life. Becoming more self-supportive, the
importance of maintaining the stability of any given
marriage may well decrease as employment provides
females with greater options, in terms of self-

validation as well as financial rewards. Levinger and Moles (1976) have referred to these various structural influences associated with greater levels of marital instability as contextural conduciveness.

This tendency to begin seeking validation of self from areas outside the institution of marriage was demonstrated by our female respondents utilizing 'single time'. Most of these respondents had traditionally viewed the marriage and husband as the primary source of validation until, after several marriages, they began to alter conceptualizations of self and develop a sense of self which was less dependent on a spouse for fulfillment. Should the present economic situation continue on at its present rate of decreasing spending power, it may well force more women to enter the labor market, to find validation of self through work and create a rising consciousness in terms of power arrangement within the marital arrangement. Should this prove the case, then there is an increased likelihood that divorce rates will rise as women perceive increased alternatives to remaining in unhappy marriages.

Spanier and Glick (1981) have also shown an association between the presence of children and the likelihood to divorce. According to their studies, the absence of children tends to increase the chances of separation or divorce and that having children tends to decrease the chances of separation or divorce. As noted earlier in the text, multiple marriers have a surprisingly small number of children given the early ages at which they married and were thus placed in a position to begin bearing children. However, emerging from the interviews with the respondents is the notion that not having children may be associated, at least for females, with an increased desire to marry. Given the exploratory nature of this study, it is not clear the effect children may have on the decision to redivorce.

Several researchers have noted that marital stability, particularly for individuals engaged in remarriage, may be dependent on an adequate pool of eligibles (Dean and Gurak, 1978; Gurak and Dean, 1979; Norton and Glick, 1981; Mueller and Pope, 1977). Multiple marriers themselves have a tendency to describe the process of appropriate mate selection as luck or chance and, to a certain extent, their conceptualizations may not necessarily be erroneous. A dwindling pool of eligibles would have the tendency to produce less homogamy among spouses, and as Glick (1975) has pointed out, "a certain amount of divorce undoubtedly grows out of the fact that the supply of acceptable marriage partners is very often quite limited (p. 10).

The Likelihood of Increased Serial Marriage

As previously mentioned, any variables which affect a rise in divorce rates for one time married spouses will necessarily cause a spillover into rates of multiple marriage. The divorce experience is indeed a learning experience and once an individual has learned the ropes, so to speak, divorce is an easier task to take on the second and third time than the initial time. One has learned how to maneuver through the legal, emotional, and social obstacles more quickly and divorce becomes less a cost and, for some persons, more of a reward. Given the growing normative support for divorce, in terms of alternative family forms, lowering of expectations regarding one time marriage as a lifetime choice, and an ideology which stresses validation of self outside the home, divorce rates may well rise. An association between these factors and an unstable economy, a situation which may force a decline in advanced education and earlier entry into the labor force for both men and women, may well prove to be the starting point for a renewed surge in divorce.

However, in attempting to present a framework with which to analyze the future of multiple marriage in society, the various related variables, socio-economic status, educational levels, median age of first marriage, role of the female in society, expectations surrounding the role of marriage in society, an unstable economy, all join together to form what appears to be a rather formidable cultural directive to society for increased divorce rates. However, the intent of this analysis was not to show to what extent the American family is dependent on society at large for its form and meaning, for the notion of family is dynamic as well as static.

The concept of family implies a process, a posturing which is dependent on a certain give and take, an influencing as well as being influenced. The family, and marriage as a social relationship, is transformed into a social unit which, in a sense, engages in a communication with society, while co-existing as part of that society. The family, in effect, becomes part of a larger societal interaction, a socially shared object, whose nature is dependent on the definitions utilized for describing it and the meanings which emerge out of the various ways people act towards it. In this sense, there is no set idea for what constitutes family or what constitutes the various conditions under which multiple marriage will increase. While viewing the family as a social object may immediately connotate a certain expectation for a common pattern of human activity (Blumer, 1969), the whole notion of family is dependent on the individuals who constitute that social object and the society which recognizes it as such.

Marriage, as it is experienced today, can be seen as both an active and passive agent in society. It is a social object with readily observable boundaries but whose nature is fluid, changable, and therefore not given to easy, dogmatic classification or pre-diction. The family, like the individuals who com-prise it, are inseparable from society and are mutually influenced by one another.

Perhaps the most basic element in the image is the idea that the individual and society are inseparable units. While it may be possible to separate the two units analyti-cally, the underlying assumption is that a complete understanding of either demands a complete understanding of the other. Coupled with this assumption is the belief that the inseparability of the individual and society is defined in terms of a mutually interdepen-dent relationship, not a one-sided, deter-ministic one. (Meltzer, Petra and Reynolds, 1975, p. 2).

In essence, while certain variables at work in society today may dictate a future marriage pattern which focuses on increased divorce and multiple marriage, the result may not necessarily be as predicted. Those individuals who comprise the social unit of a family may emerge from an interaction with society with a meaning for marriage and family life in America which will deny the directives being issued from society at large. In short, multiple marriage should not be

regarded as a mere "automatic application of established meanings, but as a formative process in which
meanings are used and revised as instruments for the
guidance and formation of action" (Blumer, 1969, p. 5).

Future Areas of Research in Multiple Marriage

In the preceding paragraphs, this researcher has
attempted to present multiple marriage as a process.
Throughout the course of this research, this researcher
has attempted to show how multiple marriage is defined
by those who participate in it. In essence, the
initial beginnings for any concentration on multiple
marriage must necessarily conceptualize marriage as an
activity, the meaning of which becomes altered through
the process of interaction with others. By observation
of those who engage in this process, it will be possible to see how the meaning of multiple marriage evolves,
is modified through interaction, interpreted differentially and is expressed in behavior. This research
has been a starting point for that study. More
involved study, in terms of replication and validation,
determination of intervening variables, is now called
for.

Certain sub-areas in the study of multiple marriage
emerged as being potentially important in understanding
the meaning of multiple marriage throughout the course
of this research effort. Conceptualizations of self
and social identity proved to be most problematic for
the participants in this research. One area of fruitful study may well be the notion of self as expressed
through marriage in a changing society.

Another interesting area may also be those aspects
of interpersonal life best studied through a drama-
turgical perspective. Multiple marriers, for a variety
of reasons, are not good team players. They appear to
have great difficulty in sustaining a joint activity.
The extent to which multiple marriers can maintain
team memberships in other aspects of social life might
prove to be invaluable in coming to grips with their
poor showing in the marriage arena.

The notion of "single time" is invested with
conceptualizations of self, however, arising from a
renewed sense of self appears to be an alteration in
the dependency on a mate for validation of self. From

this perspective, exchange theory may prove useful in coming to grips with the ways in which multiple marriers perceive marriage as a valid choice among other options. For these individuals, divorce may be the result of a process revolving around costs and rewards of marriage.

In the opinion of the researcher, multiple marriage lends itself well to future research utilizing several theoretical perspectives and varying methodological approaches. This initial attempt is seen as a starting point, a beginning. It is hoped that the approach utilized for data gathering and presentation aids in the understanding of multiple marriage as a process. It is not a definitive answer to all the questions surrounding multiple marriage, but rather a way of making that which was only "known about" somehow just a bit more "known".

REFERENCES

Albrecht, Stan L.
    1979 "Correlates of marital happiness among the
          remarried." Journal of Marriage and the
          Family (November) 41(4):856-867.

Babbie, Earl R.
    1979 The Practice of Social Research. Calif:
          Wadsworth Publishing Corp.

Bardwick, Judith and Elizabeth Douran
    1977 "Ambivalence: the socialization of women."
          The Family: Functions, Conflicts and
          Symbols. Phillipines: Addison-Wesley
          Publishing Company Inc.

Berger, Peter and Hansford Kellner
    1974 "Marriage and the construction of reality."
          Life as Theater: A Dramaturgical Source-
          book. Chicago: Aldine Publishing.

Berger, Peter and Brigitte Rose
    1979 "Becoming a member of society." Sociali-
          zation and the Life Cycle. New York: St.
          Martin's Press.

Berman, Ellen M.; William R. Miller; Neville Vines;
    and Harold L. Lief
    1977 "The age 30 crisis and the 7-year-itch."
          Journal of Sex and Marital Therapy 3(3):
          197-204.

Bernard, Jesse
    1956 Remarriage. New York: Dryden Press.

    1973 The Future of Marriage. New York: Bantam
          Books.

Bier, William C. (Ed.)
    1965 Marriage: a psychological and moral
          approach. New York: Fordham University
          Press.

Bitterman, Catherine
    1968 "The multimarriage family." Social Case-
          work (49):218-221.

Blood, Robert and Donald Wolfe
    1960 Husbands and Wives: The Dynamics of
          Married Living. Glencoe: Free Press.

Blumer, Herbert
    1969 Symbolic Interactionism. New Jersey:
          Prentice Hall.

Bogdan, Robert and Steven J. Taylor
    1975 Introduction to Qualitative Research
          Methods. New York: John Wiley and Sons.

Bohannon, Paul (Ed.)
    1970 Divorce and After. New York: Doubleday
          and Company.

Brandwein, Ruth A., C. A. Brown, and E. M. Fox
    1974 "Women and children last: the social
          situation of divorced mothers and their
          families." Journal of Marriage and the
          Family (August) 36 (3):498-514.

Brisset, Dennis and Charles Edgley
    1974 Life as Theater: A Dramaturgical Source-
          book. Chicago: Aldine Publishing Company.

Brown, C., R. Feldberg, E. Fox and J. Kohen
    1976 "Divorce: chance of a new lifetime."
          Journal of Social Issues 32:119-123.

Bumpass, L. and Sweet, J.
    1972 "Differentials in marital instability:
          1970." American Sociological Review (37):
          754-766.

Burgess, E. W. and Paul Wallin
    1953 Engagement and Marriage. Philadelphia:
          J. B. Lippincott.

Cherlin, Andrew
    1978 "Remarriage as an incomplete institution."
          American Journal of Sociology 84(3):634-649.

Chester, Robert
    1978 "Marital stability and social mobility."
          International Journal of Sociology of the
          Family 8:159-170.

Chiriboga, David, J. Roberts and J. A. Stein
    1978 "Psychological well-being during marital
          separation." Journal of Divorce 2(1):21-36.

Cleveland, Martha
    1979 "Divorce in the middle years: the sexual
          dimension." Journal of Divorce 2(3):255-262.

Chodorow, Nancy
1971 "Being and doing: a cross cultural exami-
nation of the socialization of males and
females." Women in Sexist Society: Studies
in Power and Powerlessness. New York:
Basic Books.

Dawling, Colette
1981 The Cinderella Complex: Women's Hidden
Fear of Independence. New York: Summit
Books.

Day, Randal and Wade Mackey
1981 "Redivorce following remarriage: a re-
evaluation." Journal of Divorce 4(3):39-
47.

Dean, Gillian and Douglas T. Gurak
1978 "Marital homogamy the second time around."
Journal of Marriage and the Family 40(3):
559-569.

Duberman, Lucile
1975 The Reconstituted Family. Chicago:
Nelson-Hall.

1976 "The remarried dyad." International
Journal of Contemporary Sociology 13(1&2):
93-105.

Faber, Bernard
1964 Family: Organization and Interaction.
San Francisco: Chandler Publishing Co.

Friday, Nancy
1977 My Mother Myself. New York: Dell
Publishing.

Fontana, Andrea
1977 The Last Frontier: The Social Meaning of
Growing Old. Beverly Hills: Sage
Publishing.

Furstenberg, Frank Jr.
1979 "Recycling the family: perspectives for a
neglected family form." Marriage and
Family Review 2(3):12-22.

1980 "Reflections on remarriage." Journal of
Family Issues 1(4):443-453.

Garfinkel, Harold
    1956 "Conditions of successful degradation
          ceremonies." American Journal of Sociology
          61:420-424.

Garfield, Robert
    1980 "The decision to remarry." Journal of
          Divorce 4(1):1-10.

Glasser, Paul and Elizabeth Navarre.
    1965 "The problems of families in the AFDC
          program." Children (July) 12:151-157.

Glenn, Norval
    1975 "The contribution of marriage to the
          psychological well-being of males and
          females." Journal of Marriage and the
          Family 37(3):594-599.

    1981 "The well-being of persons remarried after
          divorce." Journal of Family Issues 2(1):61-
          75.

_____, and Charles N. Weaver
    1977 "The marital happiness of remarried
          divorced persons." Journal of Marriage and
          the Family (May) 39:331-337.

Glick, Paul
    1975a "Some recent changes in American families."
          Current Population Reports. Series P-23.
          No. 52.

    1975b "A demographer looks at American families."
          Journal of Marriage and the Family 31:15-26.

    1978 "The future of the American family." U.S.
          Bureau of the Census, Current Population
          Reports, Series P-23, No. 78 (November):1-6.

    1980 "Remarriage: some recent changes and
          variations." Journal of Family Issues 1(4):
          455-478.

_____, and A. Norton
    1971 "Frequency, duration and probability of
          marriage and divorce." Journal of Marriage
          and the Family (May) 2:307-317.

1973 "Perspectives on the recent upturn in divorce and remarriage." Demography 10(3): 301-314.

1976 "Number, timing and duration of marriages and divorces in the U.S.: June, 1975, Current Population Reports.

1977 "Marrying, divorcing and living together in the United States today." Population Bulletin 32(5).

Goffman, Erving
1963 Stigma. New Jersey: Prentice-Hall.

1969 The Presentation of Self in Everyday Life. New York: Doubleday and Company, Inc.

Goetting, Ann
1981 "Divorce outcome research." Journal of Family Issues 2(3):350-378.

1982 "The six stations of remarriage: some developmental tasks of remarriage after divorce." Family Relations 31(2):213-222.

Goode, W. J.
1956 Women in Divorce. Glencoe: Free Press.

1956 After Divorce. Illinois: Free Press.

1962 "Marital satisfaction and instability: cross-cultural class analysis of divorce rates." International Social Science Journal 14:507-526.

1963 World Revolution and Family Patterns. New York: The Free Press.

Gordon, Michael (Ed.)
1978 The American Family in Social-Historical Context. New York: St. Martin's Press.

Gurak, Douglas and Gillian Dean
1979 "The remarriage market: factors influencing the selection of second husbands." Journal of Divorce 3(2):161-172.

Hayes, Maggie, Nick Stinnett, John Defrain
1980 "Learning about marriage from the divorced." Journal of Divorce 4(1):23-29.

Herman, S. J.
    1974   "Divorce: a grief process." Perspectives
            in Psychological Care 12:108-112.

Hunt, Morton
    1966   The World of the Formerly Married. New
            York: McGraw Hill.

_____, and B. Hunt
    1977   The Divorce Experience. New York: McGraw-
            Hill.

Jones, Shirley
    1978   "Divorce and remarriage: a new beginning."
            Journal of Divorce 2(2):217-227.

Journard, Sidney
    1975   "Marriage is for life." Journal of Marriage
            and Family Counselors (July) 1(3):199-208.

Klapp, Orrin
    1974   "Sources of identity problems." Life as
            Theater: A Dramaturgical Sourcebook.
            Chicago: Aldine Publishing Company:43-53.

Komarovsky, Mira
    1962   Blue-Collar Marriage. New York: Vintage
            Book, 1962.

Koo, Helen P. and C. M. Suchindran
    1980   "Effects of children on women's remarriage
            prospects." Journal of Family Issues 1(4):
            497-515.

Krantzler, Mel
    1973   Creative Divorce. New York: Evans and
            Company.

Kraus, Sharon
    1979   "The crisis of divorce: growth promoting
            or pathogenic?" Journal of Divorce 2:107-
            119.

Landis, Paul H.
    1950   "Sequential marriage." Journal of Home
            Economics (October) 42:625-628.

Laner, Mary Riege
    1978   "Love's labors lost: a theory of marital
            dissolution." Journal of Divorce (Spring)
            1(3):213-232.

Lasch, C.
    1977   Haven in a Heartless World: The Family
            Beseiged. New York: Basic Books.

Lederer, William J. and Don Jackson
    1968   The Mirages of Marriage. New York: W. W.
            Norton and Co.

Levinger, George
    1965   "Marital cohesiveness and dissolution: an
            integrative review." Journal of Marriage
            and the Family 27:19-28.

    _____, and Oliver Moles
    1976   "In conclusion: threads in the fabric."
            Journal of Social Issues 32(1):193-207.

    1979   Divorce and Separation: Context, Causes,
            and Consequences. New York: Basic Books.

Lofland, John
    1971   Analyzing Social Settings. California:
            Wadsworth Publishing Co.

McAllister, Robert J.
    1965   "Role expectations in marriage." Marriage:
            A Psychological and Moral Approach. New
            York: Fordham University Press.

McCarthy, James and Jane Menken
    1979   "Marriage, remarriage, marital disruption
            and age at first birth." Family Planning
            Perspectives 11(1):21-30.

McCrary, James
    1975   Freedom and Growth in America. California:
            Hamilton Publishing Company.

Manis, Jerome G. and Bernard W. Meltzer (Eds.)
    1972   Symbolic Interaction: A Reader in Social
            Psychology. Boston: Allyn & Bacon, Inc.

Mead, Margaret
    1947   "What is happening to the American family?"
            Journal of Social Casework 28:326.

    1966   "Marriage in two steps." Redbook, 127:48-49.

Meltzer, Bernard N., John W. Petras, Larry Reynolds
    1975   Symbolic Interactionism: Genesis,
            Varietiest, and Criticism. London:
            Routledge and Kegan Paul.

Mills, C. Wright
    1959   The Sociological Imagination. London:
            Oxford University Press.

Monaham, Thomas
    1952   "How stable are remarriages?" American
            Journal of Sociology 58:280-288.

    1959   "Marriages and migratory types." Marriage
            and Family Living (May):134-138.

Mueller, Charles W. and Hallowell Pope.
    1977   "Marital instability: a study of its
            transmission between generations."
            Journal of Marriage and the Family (Feb.)
            39(1):83-93.

Nilson, Linda Burzotta
    1976   "The social standing of a married woman."
            Social Problems 23(5):581-592.

Norton, Arthur and Paul Glick
    1976   "Marital instability: past, present and
            future." Journal of Social Issues 32(1):
            5-21.

Nye, F. Ivan
    1979   "Choice, exchange, and the family."
            Contemporary Theories About the Family.
            New York: The Free Press.

O'Neill, William
    1978   Divorce in the Progressive Era. The American
            Family in Socio-Historical Perspective.
            New York: St. Martins Press.

Oppenheimer, V. K.
    1977   "Divorce, remarriage and wives' labor force
            participation." Paper presented at Annual
            Meeting of ASA.

Parsons, Talcott and Robert Bales
    1955   Family, Socialization and Interaction
            Process. Glencoe: Free Press.

Peters, John F.
    1976   "A comparison of mate selection and
            marriage in the first and second marriages
            in a selected sample of the remarried
            divorced." Journal of Comparative Family
            Studies 7(3):483-491.

Price-Bonham, Sharon, and Jack Balswick
    1980   "The non-institutions: divorce, desertion,
            and remarriage." Journal of Marriage and
            the Family 42(4):959-972.

Richardson, John G.
    1979   "Wife occupational superiority and marital
            troubles: an examination of the hypothesis."
            Journal of Marriage and the Family
            (February) 41(1):63-72.

Riesman, David
    1950   The Lonely Crowd. New Haven: Yale
            University Press.

Riley, Lawrence and Elmer Spreitzer
    1974   "A model for the analysis of lifetime
            marriage patterns." Journal of Marriage
            and the Family 35:64-70.

Robboy, Howard, S. Greeblatt, and C. Clark
    1979   Social Interaction: Readings in Sociology.
            New York: St. Martin's Press.

Rose, Peter I. (Ed.)
    1979   Socialization and The Life Cycle. New
            York: St. Martin's Press.

Rose, Vicki L. and Sharon Price-Bonham
    1978   "Divorce adjustment: a woman's problem?"
            Family Coordinator (July) 22:291-297.

Rubin, Lillian Brislow
    1976   Worlds of Pain. New York: Basic Books.

Satir, Virginia
    1967   "Marriage as a statutory five year renewable
            contract." Paper presented at APA 75th
            Annual Convention, Washington, D.C.,
            September 1.

Schlesinger, Benjamin
    1970   "Remarriage as family organization for
           divorced persons--a Canadian study."
           Journal of Comparative Family Studies 1(1):
           101-118.

Schram, Rosalyn Weinman
    1979   "Marital satisfaction over the family life
           cycle: a critique and proposal." Journal
           of Marriage and the Family (February) 41(1):
           7-12.

Schwartz, Anne C.
    1968   "Reflections on divorce and remarriage."
           Social Casework (April):213-217.

Seward, Rudy Ray
    1978   The American Family: A Demographic History.
           California: Sage Publications.

Shibutani, Tamotsu
    1955   "Reference groups as perspectives." Ameri-
           can Journal of Sociology (May)LX:562-569.

Singh, B. Krishna, Larry D. Adams, and David E.
    Jorgenson
    1978   "Epidemiology of marital unhappiness."
           International Journal of Sociology of the
           Family (July-Dec.) 8:207-218.

Smart, Laura S.
    1977   "An application of Erikson's theory to
           the recovery-from-divorce process."
           Journal of Divorce 1(1):67-79.

Spanier, Graham B.
    1981   "The status of American families." Educa-
           tional Horizons 59(2):84-87.

_____, and Paul C. Glick
    1980   "Paths to remarriage." Journal of Divorce.
           (Spring) 3(3):283-298.

    1981   "Marital instability in the United States:
           some correlates and recent changes."
           Family Relations 30(3):329-338.

_____, and Robert F. Casto
    1979   "Adjustment to separation and divorce: an
           analysis of 50 case studies." Journal of
           Divorce (Spring) 2(3):241-253.

Springer, Joel, David Mangen and Suzanne Springer
    1974 "Relational analysis of the multidivorced,
          remarried." Paper presented at the annual
          meeting of the American Association of
          Marriage and Family Counselors of Toronto,
          Canada.

Stein, Peter J. (Ed.)
    1981 Unmarried Adults in Social Context. New
          York: St. Martin's Press.

Stryker, Sheldon
    1959 "Symbolic interaction as an approach to
          family research." Marriage and Family
          Living (May) 21:111-119.

Toffler, Alvin
    1970 Future Shock. New York: Random House.

Udry, J. Richard
    1966 The Social Context of Marriage. Philadelphia
          and New York: J. B. Lippencott Company.

U. S. Bureau of the Census
    1975 "Some recent changes in American families."
          by Paul Glick. Series P-23. No. 52.
          Washington D.C., Government Printing Office.

    1976 "Number, timing and duration of marriage
          and divorces in the United States." Current
          Population Reports Series P-20, No. 297.

    1977 "Marriage, divorce, widowhood and remarriage
          by family characteristics." Current Popula-
          tion Reports, Series P-20, No. 312.

    1978 "Historical trends." Current Population
          Reports, Series P-23, No. 70, Washington,
          D. C.: Government Printing Office.

    1978 "Marital status and living arrangements."
          Current Population Reports. Series P-20,
          No. 338.

    1978 "Perspectives on American husbands and
          wives." Current Population Reports, Series
          P-23, No. 77.

    1978 "The future of the American family."
          Current Population Reports. Series P-23,
          No. 78, by Paul Glick.

1979   "Divorce, child custody, and child support."
      Current Population Reports. Series P-23,
      No. 84.

1979   "Demographic, social and economic profile
      of states." Current Population Reports,
      Series P-20, No. 334.

1979   "Households and families by type." Current
      Population Reports Series P-20, No. 345.

1980   "Marital status and living arrangements."
      Current Population Reports. Series P-20,
      No. 349.

1930   "Marital status and living arrangements."
      Current Population Reports. Series P-20,
      No. 349.

1980   "Child support and alimony." Current
      Population Reports Series P-23, No. 106.

1981   "Marital status and living arrangements."
      Current Population Reports Series P-20,
      No. 365.

Waller, Willard
    1930   The Old Love and the New. New York:
          H. Liveright.

Weigert, Andrew J. and Ross Hastings
    1977   "Identity loss, family and social change."
          American Journal of Sociology 82(6):1171-
          1185.

Weinsarten, Helen
    1980   "Remarriage and well-being: national survey
          evidence of social and psychological
          effects." Journal of Family Issues 1(4):
          533-559.

Weiss, Robert S.
    1975   Marital Separation. New York: Basic Books.

Westoff, Leslie
    1975   The Second Time Around: Remarriage in
          America. New York: Viking Press.

    1975   "Two-time winners." New York Times
          Magazine (August) 10:10-15.

Whiteside, Mary F. and Lynn S. Auerbach
    1978   "Can the daughter of my father's new wife
            be my sister?" Journal of Divorce 1(3):
            271-283.

Winch, Robert F.
    1971   The Modern Family (3rd ed). New York:
            Holt, Rinehart and Winston.

Wiseman, Reva S.
    1976   "Crisis theory and the process of divorce."
            Social Casework 56:205-212.

YanKelovich, Daniel
    1981   "New rules in American life: searching for
            self-fulfillment in a world turned upside
            down." Psychology Today (April):67-84.

Zeiss, Antonette, Robert Zeiss and Stephen Johnson
    1980   "Sex differences in initiation of and
            adjustment to divorce." Journal of Divorce
            4(2):21-34.